Escondido
A Pictorial History of the Hidden Valley

By Robin Fox & Carol Rea

Published by HPNbooks, a Division of Ledge Media, Jackson, Wyoming

Legacy Sponsors

Through their generous support, the following companies helped make this project possible.

ALHISER-COMER MORTUARY
225 South Broadway
Escondido, California 92025
760-745-2162
www.alhiser-comer.com

KEN BLANCHARD COMPANIES
125 State Place
Escondido, California 92029
760-489-5005
www.kenblanchard.com

TOYOTA OF ESCONDIDO
231 East Lincoln Parkway
Escondido, California 92026
760-300-1112
www.toyotaescondido.com

THE HILLEBRECHT/EMERSON/ADAMS FAMILIES

Second Edition
Copyright © 2023 HPNbooks

All rights reserved. No part of this book may be reproduced in any form or by any means, electronic or mechanical, including photocopying, without permission in writing from the publisher. All inquiries should be addressed to Ledge Media, P.O. Box 230054, Encinitas CA 92023. Phone (800) 939-5311, www.hpnbooks.com.

ISBN: 978-1-944891-79-4
LCCN: 2023942575

Escondido: A Pictorial History of the Hidden Valley
authors: Robin Fox, Carol Rea
cover artist: Gloria Warren
managing editor: Daphne Fletcher
contributing writers for "Sharing the Heritage": Kevin Kern, Marcus Matthew, Sid Shapira

HPNbooks/Ledge Media
publisher & CEO: Daphne Fletcher
VP & Director of IT: Rafael Ramirez
administration: Donna Mata, Kristin T. Williamson
production: Colin Hart, Christopher D. Sturdevant

A view of Escondido from the veranda of the Escondido Hotel, looking west, in 1910.

This book is dedicated to past, present and future pioneers of Escondido.

Contents

ACKNOWLEDGMENTS 5

PREFACE 6

INTRODUCTION 7
   Jeffrey R. Epp

CHAPTER 1 — EARLIEST ESCONDIDO..8
   The Beginning of the Story, Changing Landscapes

CHAPTER 2 — COMMUNITY..28
   Housing, Faith, Education, Historic Preservation,
   Clubs & Organizations, Sports, Events, People

CHAPTER 3 — COMMERCE 60
   Transportation Industry, Agriculture, Communications, Banks, Retail & Services

CHAPTER 4 — CULTURE 86
   Music, Visual Arts, Performing Arts, Literature, Museums

CHAPTER 5 — GOVERNMENT SITES & SERVICES 99
   Buildings, Parks, Law Enforcement, Fire Protection

ESCONDIDO TIMELINE 118

SHARING THE HERITAGE INTRODUCTION 124
   Kristen Gaspar

SHARING THE HERITAGE 125
   Quality of Life, The Marketplace, Building a Greater Escondido, Family Heritage

SPONSORS 241

ABOUT THE AUTHORS 244

ABOUT THE COVER 245

ABOUT THE CONTRIBUTING PHOTOGRAPHERS 246

ESCONDIDO AND THE CORONAVIRUS 247

Acknowledgments

As the pages of this book suggest, Escondido has proven itself to always have been a community that comes together for positive efforts and to help when needed. Many persons assisted in putting this book together and we appreciate them all, starting with the community members who have graciously donated their family photographs to the Escondido History Center over the years. We thank the City of Escondido for supporting this project, including City Manager Jeff Epp, Joanna Axelrod, Vince McCaw, Raymond Seraile, Michelle Geller, Teresa Collins, Rick Vogt, Craig Carter, Ed Varso, Joyce Masterson and Linda Loughnane. Additionally, we are grateful for the time, effort and support provided by Edith Hillebrecht and her late husband, Ben Hillebrecht, and to our many sponsors who made this important historical book possible.

2020 Escondido History Center Board of Directors
June Rady, President
Carol Rea, Vice President
Rod McLeod, Secretary
Bob Johnson, Treasurer
Kent Baker
Edith Hillebrecht
Tom Humphrey
Jeff Johnson
Christ Miller
Fred Miller
Victor Pestone

Preface

In 1988, in celebration of the City of Escondido's Centennial, a book, *The Hidden Valley Heritage, Escondido's First 100 Years*, was put together by a dedicated group of local history enthusiasts, led by Alan McGrew. Since that time, a few other books have focused on specific areas of Escondido's history, but, in 2018, the Escondido History Center happened onto an opportunity to put together another book about the history of the "Hidden Valley," in order to share more of its vast collection of photographs and other resources. The result is the book you now hold in your hands, a review of our city's early history that includes rarely seen photographs from long ago, as well as a range of newer photographs with information about our more recent history. The Escondido History Center is pleased to be able to share these photographs and a glimpse into how quickly today becomes the history to be reflected upon tomorrow.

Toward the back of the book, numerous Escondido families, businesses, and organizations have financially supported the printing of this book by purchasing pages to share their own stories and supplement the historical content developed for the front. We thank them for making the publishing of this entire book possible.

What was most striking, as we put this book together, was that our city has grown and changed dramatically since its early beginnings, but it still remains a community of active and caring people who feel blessed to live, work, and play here. We hope you will also feel that sense of community and you will enjoy seeing Escondido's past, some of the present, and look forward to a continued sense of community into the future as we do.

The most challenging part of putting this book together was deciding what information and history, out of thousands of photographs and events, to include within the set number of pages. We did our very best to represent key points in Escondido's fascinating history, the story of a small town, developed by a savvy group of businessmen, as it grew to become the diverse and successful city it is today. We hope that you enjoy your step back into time.

Robin Fox

Carol Rea

Introduction

Little did I realize what was ahead when I rolled into town some thirty-three years ago. The occasion was a job interview for a deputy city attorney position. Interstate 15 was still very new. A huge subdivision was contemplated for Daley Ranch. East Valley was quiet and empty after the stores had moved to the new shopping center south of town.

My office would be in the old City Hall, which used to sit on the knoll at Grand & Valley Blvd. It's the same knoll in front of the old hospital which will soon be demolished and replaced, probably with residential buildings. Two careers later, I'm in the new City Hall, which itself is now twenty years old. Our new hospital is already six years old.

Time marches on and nearly everything changes. Yet, as I looked at an old black and white photograph of Escondido's first City Hall, I realized that the design concepts on that building had carried over to our current building. Grand Avenue and Grape Day Park have changed, but they still retain the rich, original character that make them special places in Escondido. Lake Wohlford is still a great place for fishing. The view from Bottle Peak remains awesome.

Sometimes the best way forward is pausing for a look back, and this book provides that opportunity—especially for those who have a connection with this wonderful city. As you leaf through its pages, you realize how many came before us, and they weren't all that different. You will turn the final page knowing that others will come after. And in between, you will find that Escondido history adds that sense of community, of shared friends, families, and places that make up Escondido.

I am so pleased that the City of Escondido chose to participate in the development of this book with the Escondido History Center. A city government, its citizens, and its history should be tightly interwoven. I will never forget that April evening in 1988 when hundreds of Escondido's residents filled both levels of our newly constructed City Hall to celebrate. We have always had the warmth of a small town and the benefits of a thriving city. Through the creation of this book, the Escondido History Center helps us understand that while working together creates the future, we must also acknowledge the contributions of the past. It has been a pleasure to assist them in this endeavor.

Jeffrey R. Epp
Manager, City of Escondido

Escondido 2019 City Council

From left to right: Council Member John Masson, Deputy Mayor Consuelo Martinez, Mayor Paul McNamara, Council Member Olga Diaz, Council Member Michael Morasco.

Chapter 1

The Beginning

"Escondido is the most stirring new City in Southern California...its streets are daily thronged with new arrivals, who, one and all, proclaim it the Garden Spot of the world," (November 4, 1886, *The Times*). This photograph, looking west down Grand Avenue, was taken that same fall.

The name, "Escondido" is roughly translated to "hidden place" and the city's fascinating history began on land that formerly comprised the Rancho Rincon del Diablo, an old rancho predating California's entrance into the United States. In 1886, the ranch was purchased by the Escondido Land & Town Company (EL&T Co.), headed by the Thomas Brothers; Richard, Charles, John and William, as well as Jacob Gruendike, Daniel Hale, Thomas Metcalf and several others. Numerous attempts had been made to utilize the land before, but the actions taken by the Escondido Land & Town Co. were the first to attempt to turn the area into a full-fledged city.

Escondido was just one of many Southern California towns that was established during the 1880s land boom. The EL&T Co. immediately opened a San Diego office and began building a 100-room hotel in Escondido. Proceeds from their first land sales were used to bring the railroad to Escondido, thus ensuring their community would grow and prosper.

Offering free land to anyone who would build a church or school, the young community soon had an elementary school (the Lime Street School), a large seminary built by the University of Southern California (USC) for $75,000, and several churches. The EL&T Co. also sponsored the creation of a local newspaper, *The Escondido Times*. The newspaper was used initially as an advertising tool targeting mid-western farmers, luring them to Escondido's perfect year-round growing season.

Escondido was described as one of the most prosperous and rapidly growing colonies in southern California. Two years after the EL&T Co. was formed, the city of Escondido was incorporated on October 8, 1888. Local voters approved incorporation 64-19. The population was approximately 500.

The city grew slowly but steadily, as an agricultural center ideal for grapes, citrus and later for avocados. Eventually, Escondido became the commercial center serving North San Diego County and encouraged banks and financial institutions to locate here. Both World Wars contributed to an influx of people and a labor force, light industries began moving in, and the groves and vineyards gave way to housing.

Early Escondido

In 1886, the townspeople stood in the middle of the weeds of Grand Avenue as the cornerstone was laid for the Bank of Escondido (still standing) on the northwest corner of Grand Avenue and Broadway. The Escondido Hotel is under construction on the hill in the background.

The Escondido Land and Town Company set up business first in San Diego. They then opened this office in the Bank of Escondido building in 1887. Next door was the office of the San Marcos Land Company; Jacob Gruendike was the principle stockholder in both companies.

10 ✦ ESCONDIDO: *A Pictorial History of the Hidden Valley*

A view of the Escondido Hotel under construction in 1886. When completed, the hotel had one hundred rooms and was the location of many community celebrations.

Construction of the railroad between Oceanside and Escondido began in early 1887 and was completed by the end of December that same year. This photograph was taken in the spring of 1888 before the construction of the Santa Fe Depot. A boxcar sits on a siding north of Grand Avenue.

On February 7, 1888, a sixteen-car excursion train pulled into town to celebrate the coming of the railroad. According to the *Escondido Times*, at least three housand people attended the event, which included dinner, bands from Escondido and San Diego, and a "monster" tent featuring displays of fruit

---

The construction of the Escondido depot was completed in July 1888. It was located at the very west end of Grand Avenue. In 1984, the Depot was moved to Grape Day Park and is now one of the buildings in the museum complex of the Escondido History Center. This view of the Depot was taken c. 1890.

Two little girls stand in an open field with downtown Escondido behind them. The photograph was taken c. 1894 from the northeast corner of 7th Avenue and Quince Street.

A view of Grand Avenue looking west from the Escondido Hotel (the former Palomar Hospital site) in 1895. The first building on the left is the Rainey building. The spire from the First Methodist Church can been seen just beyond. The first building on the right is the Escondido Cannery.

Chapter 1 ✦ 13

Construction began on a dam in Bear Valley in September of 1894. The Escondido Irrigation District sold water bonds to pay for the construction. The water bond debt was finally paid off on October 31, 1904. A celebration was in order and on September 9, 1905 Bond Burning Day was inaugurated. Everyone gathered in front of the Lime Street School to watch the water bonds go up in smoke.

In 1905 people came from far and near to help Escondido celebrate their "Freedom" from the water bond debt. A procession started at the train depot and went east on Grand Avenue. Every visitor went home with a basket of free grapes. This celebration was commemorated each year until 1908 when the Grape Day festival began to be held annually.

The construction of the water canal more than a century ago was the first reliable means of supplying local water to early Escondido, but led to a bitter dispute over area water rights promised by the federal government to the local Indian tribes. More than fifty years of legal battles finally gave way to an impressive example of camaraderie and teamwork between the local Indian bands and the City of Escondido that led to a historical settlement, agreeable to all parties and finalized by an act of the United States Congress in 2016.

This c.1908 photograph was taken just west of Juniper Street, between 10th Avenue and Chestnut Street, looking toward Park Hill. The Hooper House to the left still stands today at 1006 South Juniper Street.

The Beach House, built by Albert Beach in 1886 and still standing today, can be seen in this photograph taken from 8th Avenue, looking north on Juniper Street toward Grand Avenue in the early 1890s.

Fumigating citrus trees with cyanide was an early form of pest control. This c.1890 photograph shows workers fumigating the trees at the Escondido Hotel.

16 ✦ ESCONDIDO: *A Pictorial History of the Hidden Valley*

During the rainy season, fording the Escondido Creek was hazardous. A group of Escondido citizens banded together and decided to build a wooden bridge in 1889. This is a photograph of the Lime Street Bridge, at what is now Broadway near Grape Day Park, looking southeast in 1895.

The Stevenson Brothers General Merchants are making a delivery by horse-drawn wagon to this unidentified home, circa 1895. Note the dormer windows protruding from the roof of the home and the differing colors of shingles in the roof, as well as the clothing of the period worn by the family

Chapter 1 ✦ 17

Then and Now

Looking east down Grand Avenue from Tulip Street in 1903, the Escondido Hotel can be seen in the distance. The Hotel and the Train Depot were separated by a distance of one mile.

Looking east down Grand Avenue from Tulip Street in 2018, the now vacant Palomar Hospital can be seen in the distance, built on the site of the Escondido Hotel. *Raymond Seraile photo.*

Looking east along Grand Avenue from Maple Street in 1911, horses and motorized vehicles can be seen sharing the wide dirt road.

Looking east along Grand Avenue from Maple Street today reveals that the former Bank of Escondido building lost its ornate architecture over the years, but the structure, itself, remains.

Chapter 1 ♦ 19

Left: Escondido postcard c. 1950s.

On the opposite page: Harry A. Erickson took the 1936 photograph of the city and submitted hundreds of other aerial photographs to the Smithsonian Museum. Before drones with cameras became available and affordable, photographs were taken from the air through the use of balloons, kites, blimps, airplanes, helicopters, and even pigeons. The first aerial photograph was taken in 1858.

Below: Using his drone, city employee Ray Seraile took the current aerial photographs. The greatest challenges were finding the right spot to launch and photograph from and coping with trees that have grown over the years.

This aerial photograph of Escondido is also looking east, but it was taken in 2018. At the left edge of the photo-graph, the Transit Center covers the north side of the block along West Valley Parkway, with many of the old eucalyptus trees still in place. Construction equipment can be seen on the site of the former Police Headquarters near the center of the page and freight cars stand on the railroad tracks, carrying freight as they have for more than 130 years. Their destination is the silos belonging to Vitagold Brands, the only surviving poultry feed mill in the county. *Raymond Seraile photograph.*

An aerial photograph of Escondido looking east in 1936. Tree-lined Grand Avenue can be seen in the center of the bottom half of the photograph. The train depot is barely visible on the east side of the track, south of Grand. The next building to the east along Grand is a poultry and feed store, Hawthorne's Country Store today. The hill at the far end of Grand Avenue is empty after the Escondido Hotel was demolished in 1925.

An aerial photograph of Escondido looking east in 1987. The two-story Police Head-quarters can be seen slightly to the left of center and, across Valley Parkway on the left side of the photograph stands the farm workers' camp. On the right side of the photograph, the former site of the train depot can be seen as an empty lot between the grain silos and the train cars.

Chapter 1 ♦ 21

Looking northwest from the grounds of the first Escondido High School at 3rd Avenue and Hickory Street in 1915, the Schnack Apartments (later Trenton Apartments), built in 1912 at the corner of 2nd Avenue and Kalmia, can be seen in the center of the photograph.

The same view, looking northwest from the former grounds of the High School at 3rd and Hickory, incudes the Trenton Apartments, still standing on the corner of 2nd Avenue and Kalmia Street, but now obscured by trees.

22 ✦ ESCONDIDO: *A Pictorial History of the Hidden Valley*

Looking west on Grand Avenue from Ivy Street c. 1969, lots of signage, streetlights, parking meters, and traffic made the downtown a vibrant place to spend time.

Looking west on Grand Avenue from Ivy Street today reveals more trees, fewer signs, and no parking meters to give the downtown a more sedate look.

Looking south from a hillside just north of Mary Lane in 1972. San Pasqual High School can be seen under construction. The bridge over Lake Hodges can be found toward the top of the photograph.

Looking south from a hillside just north of Mary Lane in 2018. San Pasqual High School construction has long since been completed and the campus includes additional buildings. The shopping mall and Kit Carson Park can be seen to the right and residential areas can be seen covering the hillsides, surrounded by trees. *Raymond Seraile photograph.*

This plat map from 1886 shows Escondido as it was originally laid out. The Escondido Land & Town Company looked toward a future of homes, schools, churches, and ranches and created the impetus to quickly make the "Hidden Valley" a thriving town. They hired surveyor O. N. Sanford to plot Escondido townsite lots and five- and ten-acre valley ranches.

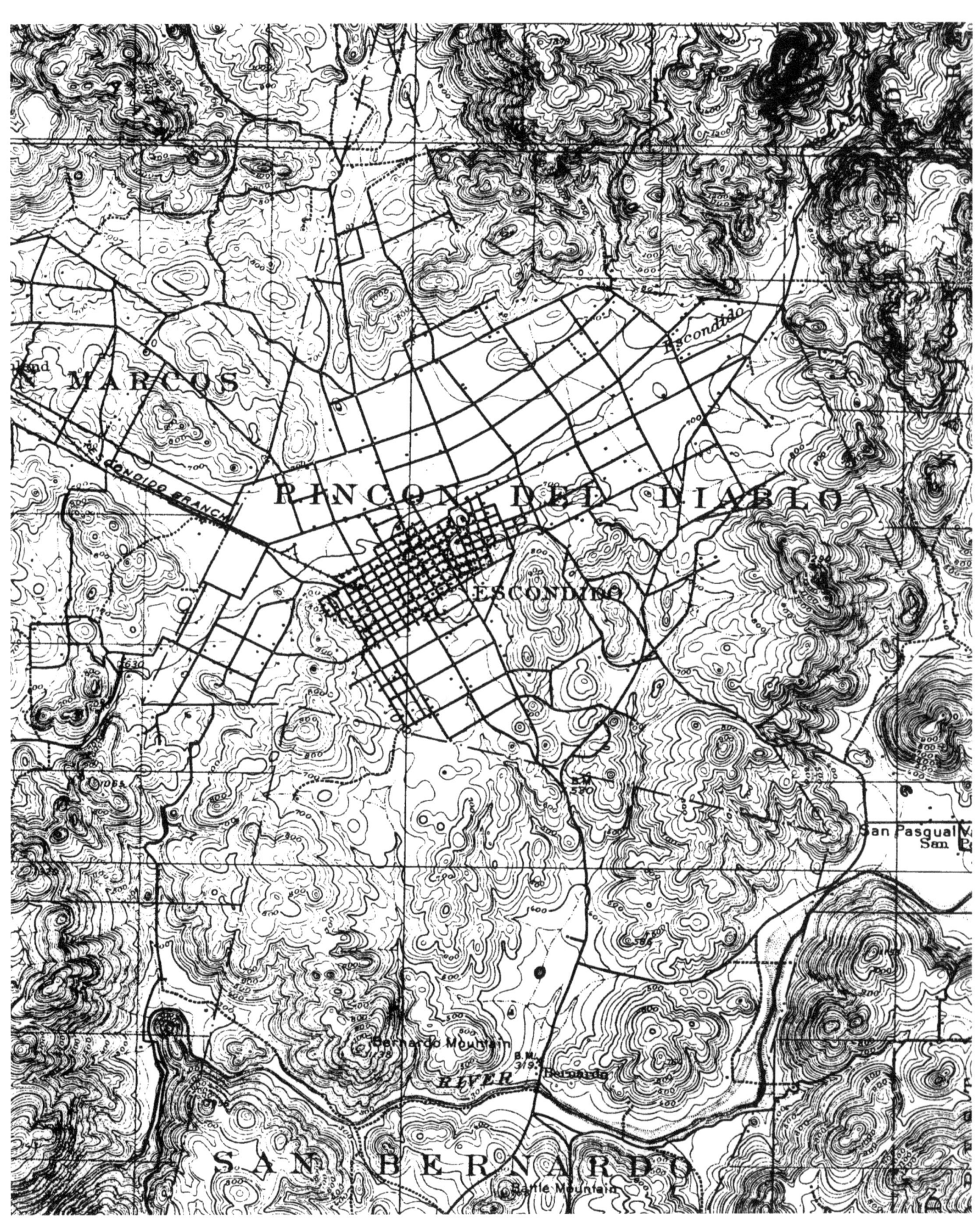

The map above shows the City of Escondido as it was in 1955. The boundaries had changed little sixty-seven years after incorporation

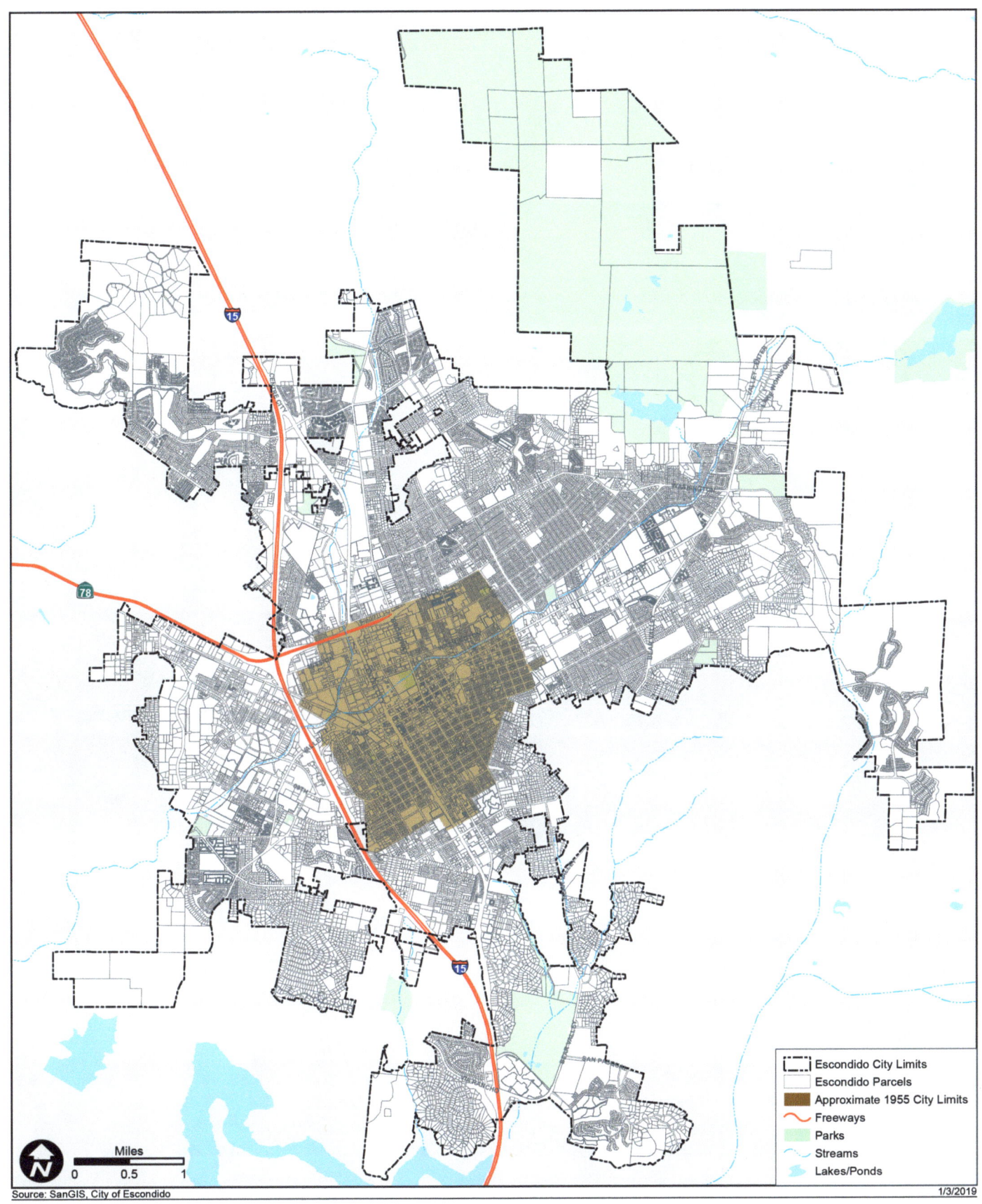

This 2018 map shows the lot lines within the city's current boundaries with the 1955 boundaries overlaid in yellow at the center. It's obvious that the City of Escondido has grown exponentially over the last sixty-four years! *Provided by the City of Escondido, Geographic Information Systems Division.*

Chapter 1 ✦ 27

Chapter 2

Community

The Escondido Duck Derby of 1942, was sponsored by the Escondido Woman's Ambulance & Transportation Corps, and was meant to raise the spirits of the community during World War II. Andy Andreasen, the City Police Judge, officiated at the event. The girls with the ducks are (from left to right): Pamela Baudy, Natalie Wilder, Leona Marin, and Eileen Beckley.

Escondido has a rich history of people of diverse cultural and ethnic backgrounds, coming together as a community and that diversity continues to be one of its strongest features today. From the beginning, when pioneering families settled in this hidden valley, it grew steadily with a boom in the 1950s and it continued growing with a population that exceeds 145,000 today. Housing for the expanding population has brought a variety of building methods and styles that has created a great diversity of neighborhoods and often among individual homes within those neighborhoods.

We are also a community of faith. The Escondido Land & Town Company donated land to churches in Escondido's early days and, since then, churches of many denominations have continued to multiply and expand here. Several significant faith-based events have occurred over the years, including the observance of the National Day of Prayer.

Schools and the way education is delivered have transitioned over the years. From the first elementary school and then the USC seminary, a strong school system has grown. Public schools and, more recently, charter schools and options for home schooling give families a wider variety of choices.

We care about our past, as well. A strong historic preservation program, instituted in 1992, created the Old Escondido Neighborhood Historic District and is protecting and preserving our built history throughout the city, while the Escondido History Center and the Library's Pioneer Room maintain vast collections of photographs, documents, and artifacts.

From the earliest times, community members came together to form clubs and organizations, offering social, networking, and community support opportunities. Community volunteers organized a variety of events over the years and sporting events, most often featuring school teams, have long been popular in Escondido.

Housing

In 1843, the Mexican government granted 12,653 acres of land—the "Rancho Rincon del Diablo"—to Juan Bautista Alvarado; the area that was to become the City of Escondido. This photograph is of the ruins of the adobe-brick built Alvarado home near present-day San Pasqual Valley Road and Bear Valley Parkway.

The Stewart House is the oldest house standing in Escondido. Alexander Stewart disassembled his two-story Eastlake-style family home, built in Nova Scotia in 1865, and shipped it around Cape Horn to Escondido. He then reassembled it in 1894 where it still stands today on 5th Avenue, near Hickory Street.

Prior to the City's incorporation, a brickyard was established along the Escondido Creek and Chinese laborers were hired to prepare the bricks for firing in the kiln. Many early structures were made out of this material because it was readily available and less expensive than lumber that had to be shipped from the northwest. This home is an example of an early structure made from Escondido brick. Built in 1885 for Charles E. Thomas and his wife, Imogene, the house still stands at 969 West 3rd Avenue.

The Thomas-Turrentine house was built circa 1885 by George V. Thomas, one of the five Thomas Brothers who founded the City of Escondido. George was the manager of the Escondido Lumber Company and Brickyard. Possibly the oldest home originally built and still standing in Escondido, it was the oldest home continuously owned by a single family in the County of San Diego, not changing hands until it was sold in 2018.

The Thomas-Turrentine House stands in this 2019 photograph with new paint colors at its original location, the northeast corner of 5th Avenue and Kalmia Street. The house was added to the National Register of Historic places in 1992 and remains on Escondido's Local Register. The original two-story Victorian period, Queen Anne-style home was altered between 1896 and 1907 with the addition of a bay window on the south side. In 1908, a Classical Revival addition was built on the east side and the second floor was expanded over the porch.

"Palma Vista" was built by L. V. Boyle on what is today Boyle Avenue and Oak Hill Drive. It later became the home of the John Whetstone family. Elsie, Roy and Clyde Whetstone are shown in the front of the house in this photograph, taken c. 1910.

In 1911, Fred and Helen Hall built a 2-½ story, Craftsman-style home with Tudor elements on 10th Avenue near Maple Street. Here, the spacious living room can be seen, decorated for a card party in 1914.

32 ◆ ESCONDIDO: *A Pictorial History of the Hidden Valley*

Many houses were built along Grand Avenue and on other streets in the downtown area in early Escondido. In 1912, local photographer Peter Schnack built Escondido's first apartment building on what is now 2nd Avenue. Built of redwood, only the city's citrus houses boasted more square footage. It featured 22 three- and four-room suites, as well as 10 single rooms, surrounding a central atrium. Renamed the Trenton Apartments after World War I, when all things German were frowned upon, the unique building still stands today.

The idea of living downtown has become popular once again, and a relatively recent plan by city leaders to create more density in the downtown area has resulted in apartments under construction and planned for the downtown area, built to house thousands of new residents. The Latitude 33 Apartment Community, at the corner of Washington and Centre City Parkway is an example of the current trend in downtown living.

The dramatic increase in population after World War II brought a housing boom to Escondido and the "mid-century" styles brought a new look to town. Mid-century modern homes with clean, simple styles, and ranch-style homes became popular. This ranch-style house was built in 1950 by B.A. Sweet, a partner in the Pine Tree Lumber Company. *Photograph by Katalin Cowan.*

Having rented a small bungalow across East 7th Avenue for nearly seven years, Bud and Cordia Sayre bought the empty lot across the street in 1946, ready to build their own home. Bud, shown in the photograph on the left, utilized Escondido granite rocks left on the lot and found elsewhere for free and learned how to split them with a weed-burning torch in order build a lovely Colonial Revival bungalow with 14-inch thick walls. The photograph on the right shows the house as it appeared in 2007.

Thanks to L.R. Green and his Adobe Block Company, the Weir Brothers and other builders were able to utilize this ancient building material, making it popular again in the mid-twentieth century. Green Ranch and Longview Acres in south Escondido were adjacent subdivisions made up entirely of adobe homes. Many others were built around the city and, as a result, Escondido has more adobe homes than any other city in California. This photograph shows adobe blocks drying at L. R. Green's adobe brickyard along Highway 395 (I-15) in 1949.

The "Castle House," built for James and Gretchen Jackson in 1964 on Palmas Avenue, is a Weir Brothers adobe home, uniquely dominated by an exterior welcoming turret. In this case, the bricks were made on site.

Chapter 2 ♦ 35

Faith

The Escondido Land & Town Company gave free land to any congregation that wanted to build a church here. Seven faiths accepted the offer and, in 1886, the Methodist Episcopal Church was the first to build, choosing the corner of Grand Avenue and Ivy Street. The church was sold in the 1920s to the first Grace Lutheran Church. Prior to being torn down in the late 1960s, the building was the home of Georgia Copeland's School of Dance.

More than three hundred San Diego County Adventists attending a conference posed for this photograph in 1914. The church, built in 1887 for a Southern Methodist congregation, was sold to the Seventh Day Adventists in 1900. In 2005, the Iglesia Monte de los Olivos, a non-denominational Latino congregation, purchased the building that still stands today on the corner of 4th Avenue and Orange Street.

The Escondido Mennonite Brethren Church, known also as Bethania Mennonite Brethren Church, was founded in Escondido in 1908 by Elder Abraham Schellenberg. The small German-speaking Mennonite colony remained in Escondido for 10 years and had a congregation of approximately 70 people. Mennonite churches are identifiable by the two entry doors; one for men and the other for women. The building was sold in 1921 and its exact location is unknown.

In 1931, a large group of Filipino workers began meeting in homes and rented halls to study the scriptures and share their new-found faith in God. By 1936 they bought and renovated a small saw-sharpening shop located at the corner of 401 West Grand Avenue and South Orange Street. The congregation named their church "Calvary Lighthouse Mission." In 1946, the congregation sold the property and constructed a new church at 950 E. Ohio Street and the church was renamed "Calvary Assembly." Unfortunately, the church was destroyed by a suspicious fire in 2014, but eventually rebuilt and reopened for services by 2018. In this 1941 photograph, the members of the Calvary Mission congregation bid farewell to their pastor.

Franklin Graham, son of well-known minister Billy Graham, launched his "Decision America." California Tour in Escondido In May 2017. Standing on a stage in Grape Day Park in front of approximately ten thousand people, Graham mentioned his early days, accompanying his famous father to Escondido when they visited friends in the area. *Photo courtesy of Billy Graham Evangelistic Association. Used with permission.*

A 4-½-ton statue of Buddha, made of rare dark jade, and valued at $5 million was displayed in Escondido in 2010 on its first stop in a U.S. tour, intended to spread peace and happiness. The 8-foot, 10-inch statue was displayed at both Grape Day Park and the Phap Vuong Monastery.

In 2010, the Escondido City Council gave a Proclamation for October 27, 2010 to be named "Day of Peace" and placed a Peace Pole in Grape Day Park. More Peace Poles followed and, as of 2018, there are 11 Peace Poles located in the City, this one located at the First United Methodist Church. The purpose of the pole is to be a symbol of the dream for Peace in our hearts, lives, homes, schools and city. The community organization, "DOVE," (Dreaming of a Violence Free Escondido) has challenged each business, organization, place of worship and school to erect a peace pole in solidarity with this message.

Education

Among the first buildings constructed in the new town of Escondido was an elementary school named the Lime Street School. Situated in what is now Grape Day Park, the Escondido Creek ran behind the school but the sandy shores of the creek did not provide an adequate foundation; the building was deemed unsafe in 1909 and torn down. A new school was built on 5th Avenue at Broadway in 1910.

Central School was built in 1938 at the site of the previously demolished Fifth Avenue School. In November 2014, Escondido voters passed Proposition E, a $181.2 million bond measure that meant new buildings and modernization for Central School, but many historical features were left intact, including murals in the multipurpose room, "cloak closets" inside the older classrooms, and the classic original look of the older buildings that allow access to individual classrooms via indoor corridors.

Built by the University of Southern California (USC) as a college in 1888, the large gothic brick building became the first Escondido High School in 1894. Because the Escondido Creek was the only place to swim at that time and it would dry up at the peak of every summer, the high school boys took it upon themselves to dig a hole, by hand, for a swimming pool that was sorely needed in this hot inland valley. It took two years for the boys to dig the hole large enough and the school board had the big basin coated with concrete in 1909. At the time, the boys and the girls of Escondido used the pool separately and this photograph of the boys cooling off in the pool was taken circa 1912.

By 1927, the first Escondido High School was no longer big enough to accommodate the growing number of students. A new high school was built that same year just down the block at 4th Avenue and Hickory Street. On the first day of class, the students walked with their chairs from the old school to the new school. This photograph shows the "new school" in 1938. This school was condemned in 1955 and a newer school, which is the current Escondido High School, was built on North Broadway.

John Paul the Great Catholic University opened in 2006 and moved to Escondido in 2013, first occupying the former J.C. Penney's store on Grand Avenue. The University has grown steadily and has purchased multiple properties along Grand and in the Downtown area, to allow more classroom space as well as housing for students seeking degree programs in communications media, business, and the humanities.

There was no Reformed seminary in the western part of the United States until Westminster Seminary California (WSC) welcomed its first students in the fall of 1980, committing itself to providing the finest in theological education. With an established a campus featuring an extensive library, a comprehensive curriculum, and a full faculty of teachers who were both experienced pastors and experts in their academic disciplines, WSC has attracted students from all over the United States and many foreign countries. *Westminster Seminary California Photograph*

Historic Preservation

By the 1980s, a heavy concentration of Escondido's earliest homes could still be found standing in the neighborhood south of Escondido's historic Downtown, but the area had fallen into serious decay and the potential for demolition posed a significant threat. With the help of Councilmember and then Mayor Doris Thurston, it was designated the city's first Neighborhood Group in 1988. The founders of the Old Escondido Neighborhood Group can be seen in the 1992 photograph on the left. Shown are (from left to right): Margaret Moir, Sharon Kramer, Doris Thurston, and Ginny Leighton. *Old Escondido Historic District Photograph.*

The City of Escondido was designated a Certified Local Government (CLG), by the California Office of Historic Preservation in 1989, after six women, all dedicated and persistent historic preservationists, spent more than eight years convincing the city to apply for the distinctive Federal preservation program. As a CLG, Escondido is responsible for designating, saving, and protecting historic structures throughout the city. In the photograph are three women who were instrumental in establishing the program (from left to right): Mable Dalrymple, Harriett Church, and Margaret Eller. Others who were vital in creating the program included Dorothy Mortensen, Meg Mount, Janean Young, and Lucy Berk.

Dedicated historic preservationist and local historian Lucy Berk served on the Historic Preservation Commission from its inception until she stepped down in 2012. Her contributions in terms of preserving Escondido's history, both in tangible structures that were saved and protected, as well as by documentation, are immeasurable.

The Old Escondido Historic District was established by the City Council in 1992 and is comprised of Escondido's oldest neighborhood, with homes in a variety of styles dating back to 1886. The neighborhood has held home tours to raise funds and awareness for more than thirty years. The photograph on the left is from June 1990. The annual Mothers Day Home Tour, as shown in the 2018 photograph on the right, has become a tradition for many families. *Photographs courtesy of Old Escondido Historic District*

Inarguably the most notable house in the Old Escondido Historic District is the Beach House, located at 7th Avenue and Juniper Street. Lovingly restored, beginning in 1998, by art dealer Harry Parashis and his wife Letitia with guidance from San Diego's Save Our Heritage Organization, the Queen Anne Victorian, built in 1896, stands out today as the Crown Jewel of Old Escondido. The Beach House is on both the National Register of Historic Places, as well as on the Local Register, here in Escondido.

Clubs & Organizations

Escondido has been the home of fraternal and service clubs over the years. In Escondido, the Kiwanis Club was the first service organization formed, just a few weeks before the Escondido Rotary Club, both having been established in 1924. This photograph shows the men of the Kiwanis Club at one of their lunch meetings at the Charlotta Hotel in 1935.

The unique East End Club was organized in 1907 by women who lived on isolated ranches at the east end of the Escondido valley and its sole purpose was to create opportunities to strengthen friendships. Remarkably, the East End Club still exists today, making it the oldest social organization in Escondido. In celebration of the club's 100th anniversary, members posed for this photograph at the Escondido History Center on May 11, 2007.

Founded in 1924, the Escondido Country Club started with a stone clubhouse and course built by the members' own hands, but the property was sold during the depression. Re-established in 1965, the manicured grass, majestic trees, and welcoming facilities of the new Escondido Country Club property provided beauty and value to create one of the most treasured neighborhoods in Escondido. The clubhouse and golf course closed in 2013 and the property was sold to a Los Angeles developer with plans to build homes. While the owners of surrounding homes and the developers continued to disagree over plans for the property, a fire destroyed the clubhouse in 2017 and the controversy continues.

Started in 2006, the Escondido Charitable Foundation's mission is to increase responsible and effective philanthropy through annual grants to charitable nonprofits serving the residents of Escondido. Through the generosity of one of its members, The Escondido Charitable Foundation is donating a community gateway arch to the City of Escondido in 2019. *Artist's conception of the Arch provided by the Escondido Charitable Foundation.*

46 ♦ ESCONDIDO: *A Pictorial History of the Hidden Valley*

The Escondido Creek Conservancy was incorporated in 1991 with a mission to preserve and restore the Escondido Creek watershed. Since that time, the Conservancy has helped preserve more than four thousand acres of land. The Conservancy also provides outdoor education programs for 3,500 youth and adults every year as in this photograph showing students releasing trout as part of the Conservancy's 2018 Trout in the Classroom program. *Escondido Creek Conservancy photograph.*

Interfaith Community Services was founded in 1979 by a handful of diverse faith communities to address the needs of low-income, homeless, and under-served people in North San Diego County. Over the years, Interfaith has evolved into a broad variety of programs and services that assist people in crisis to stabilize and rebuild their lives.

In 1989, leaders from the Escondido Union and Escondido Union High School Districts, Escondido Chamber of Commerce, and the City of Escondido formed an organization committed to developing and implementing community-wide programs to support youth, calling it Education COMPACT, for "Creating Opportunities, Making Partnerships and Connecting Teens. In the photograph from 2015, COMPACT staff and youth pose with Escondido Police Chief, Craig Carter, at the ribbon cutting of the new high visibility crosswalk at the corner of Ash Street and Mission Avenue. This crosswalk was the number-one priority identified by Mission Park residents to improve their kids' Safe Route to School. *Escondido COMPACT Photograph.*

Sports

In 1908, the Escondido High School (EHS) football team played remarkably well, considering none of the young men had played football before. EHS played San Diego's Russ High School twice and won both times. The other county team was comprised of men from the San Diego Y.M.C.A., whose members' individual average weight was greater than that of the high schoolers, but EHS held their own and lost by only four points.

This giant bonfire in 1949 was representative of school and community spirit before the annual Escondido High School football game with their rival, Oceanside High School. The week before the big game, boys from EHS would leave school early to gather wood of any kind, from trees to outhouses, and it was piled in the baseball field just west of Grape Day Park. The pep rally began at the high school campus on 4th Avenue and Hickory Street when the students held hands, formed a serpentine chain, and ran from the school down Grand Avenue to the park, where they met up with the pep band, cheerleaders, football players, and others to cheer and chant before the big bonfire was ignited.

Baseball games were played on a field at the corner of 4th Avenue and Spruce Street. Escondido's town team aided greatly in the development of several players who went on to play professionally. Outstanding among the local players were the Coscarart brothers. The oldest, Joe, eventually played for the Boston Braves, Steve played minor league baseball at Kansas City, and Pete, the youngest, played for the Brooklyn Dodgers. In this 1925 photograph are, top row (from left to right): Ted Wright, Hal Finney, Joe Coscarart, Lefty Hunt, Richard Spaulding, Sam Kolb, Dan McGrew. Bottom row (from left to right): Rupert Baldridge, Felix Quisquis, Steve Coscarart, Lloyd Babley, Dean Oliver, Marcus Alto, Pete Coscarart.

This 1941 photograph shows the "Fordettes," a local girl's baseball team that was formed to keep the baseball tradition alive in the absence of many men during World War II. The Fordettes, sponsored by Homer Heller Ford, played in an all-female league with other teams from around Southern California.

Escondido was a softball town in the 1950s and '60s. They called it Night Ball and each summer, life revolved around Finney Field, adjacent to Grape Day Park. This was the first softball field built with lights in Escondido. Watching from the stands or from an automobile was a favorite summer time activity for all ages. Finney field was named after Harold Finney, the man who helped form the Escondido Night Ball Association in 1927 and served as its president for 27 years.

The 1981 Escondido National Little League All-Stars, standing on the steps of the Escondido History Center office, were the only undefeated team that went to the Little League World Series that year in South Westport, Pennsylvania. They were the Western Little League Champions and it was the first team from San Diego County to reach the Series since La Mesa won it in 1961. Even though the team lost, when they returned home there was plenty of Little League spirit and town pride. The players were: Alex Borboa, Brett Salisbury, Russell Brooke, Frank Escalante, Nick Scales, Gary Larrabee, Bobby Esposito, Kelly Simpson, Jason Hobbs, Mike Hopkins, Peter Villalobos, Gary Kinch, and John Moran. The coach was Mike Pumar.

Events

In 1917, two circuses paraded their animals, bands and performers down Grand Avenue, two days in a row. Al G. Barnes Wild Animal Circus performed on March 9, 1917, and Cole Brothers' Big Three-Ring Trained Wild Animal Show appeared the following day. Each gave an afternoon and evening tent show, following their parade. Pictured is the Cole Brothers' troop of animals and performers. The Cole Bros. Circus was founded in 1884 and, in 1939, was the last circus to feature a horse-drawn parade. As of 2014, Cole Bros. Circus was one of the few traditional circuses in the U.S. to perform under the "Big Top" tent, but just two years later was seriously struggling, apparently in response to animal rights activists protesting the use of animals in live performances.

At each Grape Day Parade, vehicles were backed into position against the curbs along the Grand Avenue parade route so that their occupants could comfortably watch the procession pass by. The parade was a highlight of the Grape Day Festival, which began in 1908 and was in its heyday in the 1920s and '30s, when it drew up to 30,000 spectators annually. This photograph, taken from a rooftop perch, shows the parade in 1926.

Celebrating their first-place prize at the county fair, the Pio Mighetto Winery entered this float in the 1939 Grape Day Parade. The float included a cask of wine, supported by a giant mound of grapes, in addition to four beautiful young women who posed gracefully while holding the fair's first-place silver trophy above their heads.

When the Grape Day Festival was revived in 1996, Grape Day Royalty was selected using different criteria than in its early days and choices were based on service to the community. In 2003, two queens were selected, Ruth Thomas and Helen Heller, in honor of their many years of service in the Palomar Hospital Auxiliary and running the hospital gift shop.

This 2018 photograph shows the start of the 8th annual Grape Day 5K in 2018 at Grand Avenue near Orange Street; from here the participants followed the established course along Grand and south into the Old Escondido Historic District. The Escondido Sunrise Rotary Club initiated the annual 5K event, which was initially scheduled in conjunction with the Grape Day Festival, and benefits the National Multiple Sclerosis Society. More than 600 people participated in 2018, as did many spectators and local high school cheerleading squads, while the Escondido Police Department re-routed traffic.

Kit Carson Days, sponsored by the Chamber of Commerce, celebrated the opening of Kit Carson Park, in 1969. Colorado resident, Kit Carson III, 86-year-old grandson of the famed frontiersman, was invited to the festivities. This photograph shows him speaking to the crowd. The three-day festival included Square and Western dancing, a horse show, talent contest, and barbecue. The event was celebrated for the last time the following year.

In December of 2000, the Jaycees Christmas Parade celebrated its 50th anniversary with giant balloons. Rarely seen in this part of the country, the giant balloons made this landmark parade year very special. Members of local organizations were the balloon handlers with a quick hands-on training the morning of the parade. Each balloon was sponsored by a local business. "The Snowman" was sponsored by the Law Offices of Paleck & Skaja and the Escondido Rotary.

It started in 1966 with 325 lights on a young deodar cedar. Eventually, this annual Christmas display blossomed into an awesome tree with 1,800 lights and Santa's village in the front yard. John and Velma Myers decorated their front yard at 920 East 5th Avenue for more than twenty-five years and attracted multiple generations of Escondidans, as well as holiday visitors from around the world. This holiday ritual came to an end in the 1990s after John Myers passed away, ironically the same year he was slated to be the grand marshal of the Jaycees Annual Christmas Parade.

In 1988, at the invitation of Congressman Ron Packard, George H.W. Bush visited Escondido while campaigning for president. His campaign stop happened to fall in the midst of Escondido's centennial celebration and he spoke from the newly restored Santa Fe Depot in Grape Day Park. It's interesting to note that his son, George W. Bush, would also visit Escondido, 19 years later, to tour the 2007 Witch Fire disaster areas and thank the firefighters who had staged at Kit Carson Park.

On February 22, 2009, Escondido hosted the finishing leg of the Amgen Tour of California, an annual, professional cycling event on par with the Tour de France. More than 100,000 spectators gathered along the race route that day, including tens of thousands of people along Grand Avenue. The Amgen Race would return in May of 2013, when Escondido hosted the starting leg of the tour, the first time the famous race ever started in Southern California, and headed north. Again, more than 100,000 spectators lined the route to watch the cyclists and it was broadcast around the world. *This 2013 photograph provided courtesy of Amgen Tour of California.*

On Friday nights from April through September, Downtown sidewalks fill with more than 5,000 people of all ages, looking at the pre-1970s cars displayed along both sides of the streets and listening to live bands while old and new cars cruise up and down Grand Avenue. "Cruisin' Grand" was initiated by car enthusiast and local merchant Steve Waldron; the well-loved tradition started on April 7, 2000 and has brought more attention to Escondido than any other event in decades. In commemoration of 9/11, each September, Fire Truck Night brings dozens of old and new fire trucks out in full force and, high overhead, a very large American flag hangs from a fire truck's extended ladder. This enhanced photograph of one of those occasions was taken by Heidi Hart in 2013 and entered into the City's "Happy Birthday, Escondido" contest.

Also satisfying the area's hunger for vintage vehicle events, is the annual American Heritage Car Show, sponsored by the Escondido History Center. The Car Show has been bringing together enthusiasts to "park on the green" of Grape Day Park since 1997. Photograph from the 2009 event.

People

A familiar Escondido sight at the turn of the twentieth century was San Pasqual Indian princess Felicita with her husband, Boley Morales, on their donkey. In 1906, they were found destitute in an old hut in one of the canyons leading into San Pasqual Valley. Elizabeth Judsen Roberts befriended the couple, and cared for them. She eventually wrote a book, *Indian Stories of the Southwest*, based on Felicita's local accounts. Felicita died in 1916 and, in 1920, a pageant was written in her honor. A county park now bears her name as does a street and several shopping centers.

Scrap drives were a regular occurrence throughout World War II. As this delightful photograph from our archive illustrates, these youngsters managed to make it fun. Loading up scrap metal for the war effort in their wagon, made from a citrus box and bike wheels and pulled by a goat, are Tom Hinrichs, George Payne, and Jerry Smith.

Escondido's first barber, Leo Escher stands behind a wire fence with his pet goat in this c. 1910 photograph. A native of Germany, he named the goat "Glocke Baah" because of the bell that hung around its neck. "Glocke" is German for "bell." "Baah" represented the sound the goat made. Whenever Escher would sit down, this particular goat would climb up on his shoulders and Leo would walk around the property at ease, just as you see him in the photograph. With limited space on his property at 109 West 7th Avenue, Escher raised goats instead of cows for their milk and to make cheese.

Known as the "Golden Greek," Jim Londos was a professional wrestler in the 1920s, '30s, and '40s. During his career, professional wrestling was a big sport in this country, a genuine athletic event, not mere theater. A resident of Escondido for almost forty years, Londos retired from the sport as world champion in 1946

Amateur astronomer Clarence Friend looks through the lens of the 16-inch telescope that he built in his backyard orange grove. From his backyard observatory, Friend became world-renowned as the discoverer of three comets that bear his name. He was also co-discoverer of another comet and of a nova (new star) in the constellation of Puppis. His discoveries won him many accolades, including a membership in the Royal Astronomic Society of London, England; the most famous of all astronomers' groups. Upon his death in 1965, his widow donated his telescope to Palomar College.

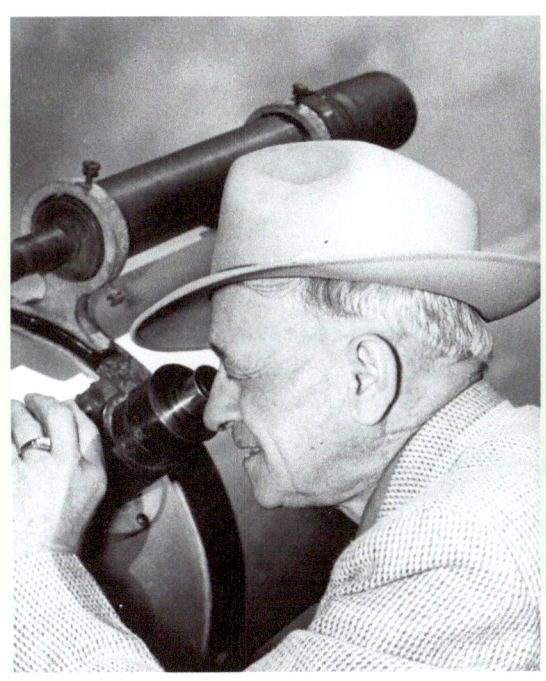

Silent movie actor Billy Beven and his dog, Spot, pose in this 1927 photograph at his ranch in southwest Escondido. Well known as one of the early movies' comical Keystone Cops, Beven purchased his 31-acre ranch in 1924 and planted 15 acres in citrus and then more in avocados. Eventually he built a home and dubbed it "Rancho La Lomita." He is credited with introducing the use of wind machines to combat frost in cold pockets of avocado and orange groves. The idea caught on and the use of wind machines was generally adopted by growers throughout the area.

Chapter 3

Commerce

Grand Avenue was a bustling, vibrant place in Escondido's early days. Businesses of all types lined the wide dirt road. This postcard, mailed in December 1911, shows the view from the 100 west block toward the east. Horse-drawn wagons share the road with automobiles and the ornate Bank of Escondido building can be seen on the corner at the left.

While the area had been farmed for many years, the Escondido Land & Town Company was Escondido's earliest commercial enterprise, a group of developers looking toward a future of other businesses, homes, schools, churches, and ranches in this Hidden Valley. They developed a clever marketing plan and it worked; a lumber company and brickyard were soon started to handle the building surge. Blacksmiths and wheelwrights like Thomas Bandy and Alexander Stewart set up businesses to repair wagons and forge hardware and tools. The hospitality industry began with the 100-room Escondido Hotel, built to accommodate the many early visitors. Later, as horse drawn wagons were replaced by automobiles, surfaced streets began to crisscross the County and by the 1940s, motor courts and motels became economical "homes away from home" for families seeing the country.

Agriculture, started on early ranchos, continued to grow along with the city. Census reports from the early 20th century reflect an influx of farmers, especially from the East, Midwest, and Europe. Families like the Hillebrechts and the Henrys ran large farms on the outskirts of town, still operating today. Grapes were Escondido's largest crop in the early days, later to be replaced by citrus fruit and avocados, but the fertile soil and mild weather meant that nearly everything could grow here. Edward Paul Grangetto, Sr., first arrived in Escondido in 1913 and, in 1952, he started Grangetto's Farm and Garden Supply, still run by the Grangetto family today.

Before the prohibition era, there were at least a dozen wineries in Escondido, but only the Ferrara Winery survived beyond that time and it continued to operate until 2011. The historic site was taken over about six years later by new owners joining multiple new wineries in and around Escondido. Also becoming popular more recently are local craft breweries, the most successful and now thriving internationally, Stone Brewing Company.

In time, other businesses needed by the growing township lined Grand Avenue in the Downtown. Pharmacies, general stores, restaurants, and markets featuring locally grown produce, brought commerce to Escondido. Services, like those provided by barbers and photographers, came along, as well.

In later years, as the town continued to grow, malls became popular. The Escondido Village Mall, the Auto Park, and North County Fair brought numerous businesses into single shopping sites to make it easier for shoppers to spend their money.

Truly diverse companies have made Escondido their home over the years. Dr. Bronner's Magic Soaps was founded in 1948 by Emanuel Bronner, a third-generation master German soapmaker, and it became a company respected world-wide; the headquarters and manufacturing plant operated here on West Mission from the 1960s until 2014 when it moved to Vista California. The Ken Blanchard Company, Escondido Disposal, and Alhiser-Comer Mortuary have all served the community for many years while relatively newer ventures like Trapeze High, a unique school for teaching the art, have also become established.

Transportation Industry

The Escondido Land & Town Company initiated the construction of a rail line from Oceanside to Escondido in 1887 for hauling freight and to bring prospective settlers to the town. The Santa Fe Depot was built near the corner of Grand and Spruce Street, where this photograph was taken around 1890. Passenger service ended in 1945 and the depot was moved to its current site in Grape Day Park in 1984 when it was no longer needed for freight storage. A freight train continues to run through the area at night. The Sprinter, a 22-mile light rail system run by the North County Transit District, re-established passenger service with 15 stops along the way to Oceanside in 2008.

The Escondido Hotel, on the knoll of East Grand Avenue was built by the Escondido Land & Town Company in 1886 and purposely located at the east end of Grand Avenue, across town from the railroad depot, to provide visitors with an opportunity to see more of the lovely Hidden Valley before reaching their accommodations. The three-story building included 100 rooms.

In this photograph from 1890, the stagecoach is carrying passengers and freight along the narrow dirt road that was the only link between San Diego and Escondido. The eight-hour trip would include a break for lunch in what is now Poway. Still unpaved by the turn of the twentieth century, motor vehicles found it a challenge, but by 1910, they would outnumber the horse-drawn wagons and the road was paved in 1920. The grade would eventually become part of Route 395, the only direct route from San Diego to the Canadian border.

The Lake Hodges Dam was completed in 1918, flooding the area, and the Lake Hodges Bridge was added in 1919. In the late 1960s, needed improvements and realignment of the road meant that the bridge was demolished and a new one built in 1969. That bridge, too, would be demolished and replaced again in 1981 when the route became I-15, and it was widened in 2006-2009. In 2009, a second bridge across Lake Hodges, built for pedestrians and cyclists, was opened slightly to the west. When built, it was the longest of its type in the world, designed for the least amount of impact on the sensitive habitats located there.

The newly built Highway 395 "freeway," as shown in this 1959 photograph, is now Centre City Parkway. The palm trees had been planted along Grand Avenue in 1914. Route 395 was designated historic by the State of California in 2008.

In 1945, railroad passenger service ended between Escondido and Oceanside. Homer Heller Company provided a station wagon to transport passengers between Escondido and Oceanside, beginning in September with four daily runs. As ridership increased, a pre-war school bus that Homer Heller whimsically labelled a "stage" came into use, later replaced by a regular transit bus.

Escondido has had three very small airports. The most significant was Engel Field, developed in 1942 by Anna von Seggern. Featuring two runways it was located on 60 acres north of what was the Talone Meat Packing plant, in the northwest part of town. Other sites for a larger airport were considered in the 1960s, but interest waned and Palomar Airport at Carlsbad was deemed close enough. Anna von Seggern, is shown in the photograph with her husband, John Engel, at the airport that bore his name.

64 ✦ ESCONDIDO: *A Pictorial History of the Hidden Valley*

Families enjoyed trips in the family car and multiple motor courts, less expensive than hotels and featuring convenient parking stalls near each unit, sprang up along the way. Several motor courts can still be found here, like this one on Escondido Boulevard.

Pine Tree Lodge-Motel
U.S. 395 & 78, Escondido, California

Pine Tree Lumber Company owner B. A. Sweet used massive redwood timbers to build the Pine Tree Motor Lodge in a western ranch style in phases, between 1953 and 1958. Located at what is now Mission and Centre City Parkway, it was the first place to settle in as travelers came into town from the north. Sweet served on the City Council and also on the County Board of Supervisors when he wasn't managing the lodge and running Pine Tree Lumber. His grandson, former state senator Mark Wyland, learned to swim in the Pine Tree Lodge swimming pool.

Located adjacent to the Pine Tree Motor Lodge, the Wagon Wheel Restaurant was a popular place to eat for locals and travelers alike from 1953 until 2014. When the Charger football team's practice field was located in Escondido during the 1960s, the team members often ate breakfast here. Numerous celebrities dined here, as well, including Robert Young, Jim Kennedy, and Dale Robertson. The "sputnik" was added to a cupola, and later plywood horses added to the roof, making the restaurant truly unique. The horses blew over in a windstorm and the sputnik mysteriously disappeared after the restaurant closed. The Wagon Wheel Restaurant and the Pine Tree Lodge were both demolished in 2017 to make room for a shopping center and carwash.

The Car Hop Drive-In Café was built in the early '40s at 314 East Grand Avenue. The place to hang out after school, games, and dances, it was so popular that cars usually parked three deep. When the first car in line was ready to leave, the two cars behind would have to pull out and then drive back in. This photograph was taken c. 1945; the business closed by 1964.

Agriculture

Agriculture was Escondido's most significant money maker in the early years. Its growth depended on the construction of the Bear Valley Dam, and the expansion of a water system was completed in 1895. In time, the formation of the Escondido Mutual Water Company stabilized the availability of water to most ranches, farms, and homes that functioned without wells. With water, the grape industry expanded.

The construction of the Escondido reservoir and canal more than a century ago was the first reliable means of supplying local water to early Escondido, but led to a bitter dispute over area water rights promised by the federal government to the local Indian tribes. More than 50 years of legal battles finally gave way to an impressive example of camaraderie and teamwork between the local Indian bands and the City of Escondido that led to a historical settlement, agreeable to all parties and finalized by an act of Congress in 2016.

Lewis B. Boyle irrigated his orange trees using a wooden water flume. His property and house were on Boyle Avenue near Midway Street and Oakhill Drive.

Grapes thrived in the Escondido soil and climate and the Muscats grown here were considered the sweetest tasting anywhere. Here, a group pauses for a photograph while picking grapes in 1910.

The Escondido Lemon Association was the largest citrus grower in the state and their packing plant, seen here in 1928, was located at Tulip and Del Dios Road. Designed in the Mission Revival style by architect J. Rex Murray, it was the largest packing house under one roof in the citrus belt. More than 800,000 field boxes of lemons were processed here annually.

Inside the Escondido Lemon Association packing house, lemons were washed and graded. Many women were employed in the plant, which was the largest employer in the city at the time. In the photo, you can see recently picked lemons packed into boxes in the fields and stacked prior to processing.

Chapter 3 ✦ 69

In addition to their packing house, the Escondido Orange Association operated this plant where ice was manufactured and stored to pack into produce transporting railroad cars before refrigeration was available. During World War II, high school students helped load ice when the regular workers were called away to war. Much of the ice plant, located on what is now Metcalf, remains there today and a later "ghost sign" is still visible.

This picking crew, made up mostly of Filipinos, worked in the groves for the Escondido Lemon Association. In addition to picking the fruit, they were responsible for planting new trees, cultivating the soil, fertilizing, pruning, and protecting the trees from frost.

When the Filipinos were drafted during WWII, Mexican Nationals were hired and a camp with kitchen and dining hall was provided at Quince and Valley Parkway, where the Transit Station is now located. Many Latino families remember the camp as the place of origin of their Escondido past. Max Atilano, foreman for the fruit picking crew, and best remembered as an entertainer, penned music for a corrido about life at the camp. This photo, most likely from the 1960s, shows the vacant buildings of the camp among the eucalyptus trees.

In the 1920s, most homes in Escondido had a flock of chickens to feed the family, but raising poultry turned into a profitable industry. Hatcheries were lucrative businesses well into the 1930s, as Escondido's population grew. Here, Ralph Squier stands with his daughter, Geraldine Squier (Beckman), in front of their chicken coop at his truck farm.

Pigs and cattle were also raised here and a slaughter house near the railroad tracks was established in the 1930s when Henry and Mario Talone opened a packing house and market on Hale Avenue, shown in this photograph from 1959. It would change hands and variety of services over the years until it was finally closed and left vacant for several years; it was destroyed by fire in 2016. Multiple dairies and creameries were located in the Escondido area over the years, as well.

The San Diego County Farm Bureau was one of the earliest farm bureaus organized in the state. The first formal meeting was held on Feb 20, 1914 at the Spreckels Theater in San Diego. Today, the San Diego County Farm Bureau is a non-profit organization supporting the more than 5,700 farms within the county. The San Diego Farm Bureau "AgHub" moved to 420 South Broadway in 2018. The Hub serves as local agriculture's key site for sharing knowledge and a place for agricultural groups to hold meetings and exchange ideas.

Communications

The *Escondido Times* was the town's first newspaper, founded in 1886 and published by Amasa Sibrent Lindsay, a Civil War veteran and experienced newspaperman and his partner, Richard Beavers. The first office for the *Times* was located on Grand Avenue, on a lot donated by Thomas Metcalf. Still standing today at 114 West Grand Avenue, it can be seen in this 1889 photograph, taken during the Decoration Day parade. The *Advocate* was founded in 1891 and it would merge with the *Times* in 1909. Through name changes and mergers, it became one of the longest-standing institutions in Escondido. In 2012, it was purchased by the *San Diego Union Tribune* and publication ended in 2013. A few free and online papers have provided news since, including *The Paper*, *The Grapevine*, and eventually, the new *Times Advocate*.

In 1952, Kay Owens started Escondido's only radio station and the call letters, KOWN, came from her name. It was first located on Hale Avenue between the Patio Playhouse's first site, and Verne Williamson's septic tank business. Alan Skuba, who would become mayor, bought KOWN in 1964 and moved it to the Escondido Village Mall on West Valley Parkway. In this photograph from 1965, on the right, Skuba is seen interviewing US Senator and former actor George Murphy in the Village Mall studio.

This photograph, from July 4, 1905, shows the entire staff of the Escondido Telephone company, which served Escondido, San Pasqual, and San Marcos. Left to right: Ed. J. Hatch, Manager; Harry Smith, "trouble shooter;" Olga McCorkle and Pearl Trumbley, operators; and "Daddy" Black, another trouble shooter. In 1919, the telephone business office moved to the corner of 2nd Avenue and Broadway and, while the names have changed, a telephone company has remained there ever since.

In 1899, the first Escondido telephone directory was published and listed 18 phone numbers. By 1955, when this photograph was taken, the number of homes with phones had increased dramatically and the phone company had many employees handling calls, before the advent of self-dialed phones. Women were considered to have more soothing voices and from early on, telephone operators were women. *Westminster Seminary California Photograph*

Banks

The first bank was the Bank of Escondido, established in 1887. During a financial downturn in 1890s, it was the only local bank to survive. Shown here in the 1890s at the Northwest corner of Grand Avenue and Lime Street (now Broadway), the building features an addition and is surrounded by the wooden boardwalk. The structure has experienced multiple changes with many details lost and covered over, but returned to a more classic look by realtor and property developer, James Crone.

Built in 1975 for the headquarters of North County Bank, this unique structure was located at the corner of 5th Avenue and Escondido Boulevard. Architect Chris Abel from Laguna Beach was responsible for the unusual design. Other tenants who did business in the building included Ken Hugins, former city treasurer for more than thirty years, and George Chamberlain, local financial expert and broadcast personality. The building also housed the headquarters of Robert Klark Graham's Nobel prize winner sperm bank. In 2000, when North County Bank merged with Wells Fargo Bank, it became a Wells Fargo branch. After Wells Fargo closed the office, the building sat empty and was allowed to deteriorate for nearly a decade except for a brief period when a church leased it, but with no plans to replace it, the building was demolished in early 2017.

Retail & Services

The Board of Trade was founded in 1886 but it was renamed the Chamber of Commerce in 1895. In 1919, ground was broken for a California mission-style building located at Grand Avenue and Maple Street. After moving to Escondido Boulevard and 5th Avenue in 1960, the Chamber would again move to the corner of Park Avenue and Broadway in 1982. They remain at that location today although the building was replaced; the new one dedicated April 19, 2005. The Chamber of Commerce has been instrumental in bringing businesses to Escondido and helping businesses succeed for 130 years.

The Avenue Livery Stable was located next door to McDonald & Rechnitzer House and Carriage Painting in the 300 block of East Grand, shown here in 1910. Horses and mules were the primary means of local transportation and Speer's Truck & Transport carried commercial items as well as household items, like the trunks loaded in the back of the wagon in the photograph.

A surprising number of women owned and operated businesses in Escondido's early days. This photograph of Mrs. Pendergast and her son, standing on the steps in front of her Chicago Millinery Store with Mrs. Stiles standing next to them, was taken around 1895.

Loomis & O'Dell sold second hand goods in a store at 237 West Grand Avenue, a building that still stands today. Their slogan, "Will trade you what you want for what you don't want—we buy everything," appeared on their Grape Day float in 1919, along with their phone number; 167-J.

From 1886 to 1896, there was only one phone in the area, located at Graham & Steiner's General Store on the southwest corner of Grand and Broadway. Graham & Steiner's was the first grocery store in Escondido and, shortly after Escondido became incorporated in 1888, they added a wider variety of stock, converting it into an early department store. The upstairs space was a community space, "Eagle Hall," but in 1960, it, like most other second floors in the downtown area, was removed out of concern for earthquake risks.

Horace Lyon was 73 years old when he built the Escondido Mercantile Company on the southwest corner of Grand Avenue and Kalmia in 1905. The 50- x 70-foot store stood on two lots and boasted a wide variety of mens and womens wear, shoes for adults and children, and sewing notions and materials. Who the legs belong to in the lower left corner of the 1905 photograph and why the person is lying in the street remains a mystery.

Ting's Pharmacy, located on the northeast corner of Broadway and Grand, was owned and operated by Darwin M. "Pete" Ting, who owned and operated the store from 1920 to 1960. The fountain inside was a popular gathering place for enjoying coffee, milk shakes, or lunch.

By 1927, when this photograph was taken, the streets downtown had been paved and striped for diagonal parking. The flag pole was installed at the intersection of Grand and Broadway on June 12 of that year, in honor of Flag Day, but it was removed in 1944 because rust had damaged its structural integrity. The pole was cut into pieces and the longest piece now stands in front of City Hall, still flying the American flag and, now, the City flag, as well.

The Downtown continued to draw considerable activity in the 1960s and the look of many of the buildings was changed to reflect the times. The building that once housed the Graham and Steiner store was "modernized" and a band of tiny mosaic tiles edged the overhang. The remarkable vertical sign at the corner makes it very clear that this was now a drugstore.

Probably the most interesting grocer in Escondido history was Rube Nelson. After buying a smaller store on Broadway with his brother in 1937, they expanded their stock until they needed a larger new store a block north at Washington. Rube became the sole owner of the "Country Corner," which sported an array of over-sized animals on the roof and grounds. Rube sold the business and property to the Albertson's chain and retired a millionaire in 1983, but, quite a character, Rube is still fondly remembered by many in the community.

Edward Woolley was a professional golfer from Scotland who began making golf clubs at the age of 12. He emigrated to the US in 1922 and, after World War II, bought Chicago-based Golfcraft. In 1952, he moved the company to Escondido where this plant was built at 1021 West Mission, bringing 22 workers and their families from Chicago to work there. Golfcraft would eventually employ a total of 167 workers and produce 600,000 golf clubs, the third largest producer of golf clubs in the United States. The company's Vice President, Edward Redmond, served on the City Council from 1955 to 1962. Golfcraft also developed and was the first company to manufacture fiberglass golf club shafts. The property was sold to the manufacturer of Titleist golf equipment in 1969 and more recently purchased by Escondido Disposal Incorporated, who adapted it as part of their state-of-the-art recycling center.

As the city grew, businesses could be found in other areas, often grouped together. These fashion show models from the Walker Scott Department Store are standing in front of the Escondido Village mall. Built in 1964, it was the first enclosed mall west of the Mississippi River, but only two decades later, it wound up in bankruptcy. A Los Angeles-based company purchased the property in 1984 and, later, when it faced stiff competition from the new North County Fair Mall, Escondido Village underwent a major renovation and turned into a strip mall, offering easier access to individual shops by their customers that has proven successful.

An aerial view looking west, with Valley Parkway running along the far-right side from the lower righthand corner, shows the old Vineyard mall, built in 1974, with its wood-clad angular buildings that housed a two-screen movie theater, a radio station and several quality restaurants. To the west of the Vineyard is the Village Mall, closer to the top of the photograph, and another strip mall can be seen to the east, toward the bottom of the photograph.

North County Fair, the largest mall in the county, boasted six anchor stores when it was opened on February 20, 1986, with confetti shot from rooftop cannons, 5,000 helium-filled balloons and seven huge hot-air balloons, cheerleaders, magicians, music makers and speeches. The mall was purchased by Australian firm, Westfield, who renamed it Westfield North County in 1998 and completely renovated the shopping mall in 2012. In 2017, Westfield Corp., including their 16 malls in California, was sold to French commercial real estate giant Unibail-Rodamco.

In 1970, five auto dealers came together as the Escondido Auto Dealers Association and they decided that Escondido should have an auto park. In 1977, two realtors were able to convince 29 separate property owners to sell their 78 acres north of Valley Parkway, east of the I-15 freeway. Today, the five posts bearing flags at the entrance to the Escondido Auto Park still represent those initial five auto dealers, and 14 automobile dealerships line the loop at "the Home of the Full Circle Test Drive."

George Weir started out by driving a pickup truck around town, filling potholes; the photograph of George is from the late 1970s or early 80s. His work ethic would lead to the development of several businesses and Weir became well known for his philanthropy. From filling pot holes for the city at no charge, to helping create the Heritage Garden at Juniper and Grand and enhancing outdoor areas at the Center for the Arts, George and his wife, Cynthia have quietly made a difference in Escondido.

The Treasure House, shown in this 1947 photograph, was located at the corner of Grand and Quince. Customers could store their frozen food here when space at home was absent or lacking in size. The building stands today and can be recognized by the curved window of glass blocks at the corner. Next to it was an earlier site for Pyramid Granite, a granite cutting factory.

The Offshore Model Basin, formerly on Enterprise Street, contained a 300-by-50-by-15-foot-deep indoor pool capable of creating significant waves. It was often used to test boats and underwater equipment by companies and organizations from around the country. It also hosted an annual submarine race for college students, as shown in the photograph, and used for making movies, including scenes from the movies *Titanic*, *True Lies*, and *Free Willy*. *Photograph courtesy of Jill Campbell.*

Stone & Glass is an art glass and mixed media studio and gallery that began in a tiny 500-square-foot studio in 2001, the culmination of James Stone's lifelong dream to be a full-time working artist. In 2015, the owners were drawn to Escondido for its history of glass arts and art culture and moved into the industrial area. Following a fire that started in a neighboring business, Stone & Glass moved into their current location on Grand where emerging artists continue to be mentored and students are taught the art. *Photograph courtesy of Stone & Glass*

Giants of Business

The Joor Muffler Man has stood steadfast on the corner of Juniper Street and Valley Parkway in the Downtown since he was placed in front of the muffler shop in the 1960s. Made of fiberglass, he stands 22 feet tall on top of a concrete base and has had quite a wardrobe through the years. Below, the Joor Muffler Man can be seen in his Santa suit, enjoying the holidays.

In addition to its unique sign in the front parking lot, the Ups 'N' Downs Roller Rink on North Broadway featured a giant roller skate on the roof. The roller skating rink was built in 1959.

The Muffler Man was wearing his Amgen vest and cap to honor the Amgen Tour of California bicycle race that started in the Downtown in 2013.

Chapter 3 ♦ 85

Chapter 4

Culture

The Escondido Band lined up for the Decoration Day parade on May 30, 1889 in front of the Methodist Episcopal Church, the first church constructed in Escondido. Barber Leo Escher can be seen on the very left, wielding a baton as the drum major.

Escondido's relationship to the arts and its endeavor for cultural development began almost at the city's incorporation in 1888. The first city band was formed by twelve local musicians. In 1889, a band stand was built on the southeast corner of Grand Avenue and Maple Street. Band concerts often made Sundays and holidays merry occasions. These early days also boasted local celebrations, eventually including the Grape Day Festival, which always had a musical component. Early theatrical productions were also quite common in the schools, churches and clubs.

In the 1920s and 30s, the Community Arts Association was organized to give attention to arts and drama. About the same time, local optometrist, Benjamin Sherman, who had studied drama at leading Southern schools, gathered local young people together and presented several plays at the Kinema Theatre. Audiences of 500 to 700 attended. Later, he wrote the outdoor play "Felicita." In more recent history, the Patio Playhouse Community Theatre has been providing local, live theatre since 1967.

In 1946, the Philharmonic Arts Association was formed and launched its first concert series, held in the Escondido High School auditorium. Through the Association's efforts, Escondido was host to world-renowned artists such as Risë Stevens, Jose Greco, Artur Rubenstein and the Los Angeles Philharmonic.

In the 1970s, the Escondido Regional Arts Council was created to bring visual arts to North County. The first gallery was in the Vineyard Shopping Center on East Valley Parkway. Today, the Municipal Gallery and the Escondido Arts Partnership both provide venues for local artists to exhibit their work.

The City established a Public Art Program in 1988 and more than 22 public art projects have been installed by the City of Escondido and private developers under the guidance of the Public Art Commission.

Also in the 1970s, the cultural history of the community came into focus with the establishment of Heritage Walk in Grape Day Park. The City's first library was identified and moved to the Walk, opening in 1976 as the first local history museum. Since that time, other historic buildings have been added to Heritage Walk to help keep the history of Escondido alive. Additional museums and galleries have been established in the City, over time, to provide the people of Escondido with well-rounded cultural opportunities.

With the success of the Regional Arts Council, a stronger, more comprehensive Felicita Foundation was formed, which successfully lobbied to use the city's old library space upon completion of the new library in the early 80s. With the support of the National Endowment for the Arts, the Felicita Foundation was able to use the newly acquired space to present both visual and performing arts in a limited scope.

Sparked by this civic vision that recognized how vital the arts are to a community, Escondido voters, in 1985, approved the building of a $73 million arts center that would bring music, dance, theater, education and the visual arts together on one dynamic campus as part of an overall redevelopment project. Since its opening in 1994, the California Center for the Arts, Escondido has been dedicated to promoting the arts along with their power for community building and enhancement, and to enrich the lives of Escondido citizens.

Literature has always played a key role for Escondido residents, as well. First librarian Mina Ward authored a book that included her own stories as well as articles from technical magazines to assist in gauging shorthand speed. Several other notable authors have made Escondido their home, including, more recently, Martha C. Lawrence and former Escondido Police Officer Neal Griffin; as well as childrens book illustrator Debbie Tilley.

Music

The Escondido Band added "Cornet" to its name and and later donned uniforms to pose for this professional photograph, c. 1890.

Max Atilano and his Mexican Troubadours were a constant at the Grape Day Festivals from 1920-1940. They also provided music for the outdoor play, Felicita. Shown in this c. 1925 photograph are (from left to right): Pete Ruiz, Frank Salcido, John Cosio, Ted Borja, Senorita Paquita Cantu, and Max Atilano.

"Sound Town" was one of the original stores in the Escondido Village Mall and one of the favorite hangouts for those who enjoyed music. This 1965 photograph shows Lawrence Welk promoting one of his albums at the popular store as the featured star of the day. Welk had a special connection to the area and visited often because of his Lawrence Welk Resort just north of Escondido. He sometimes produced his popular TV show in Escondido, which brought national exposure to the city. *Photograph by Bill Rutledge*

John Marikle built his art and music store on South Kalmia in collaboration with photographer Louis Havens, who built his photograph studio next door and took many of the early photos found in this book. Both businesses opened in 1911. Each family lived in an apartment above their respective store.

In 1970, artist Frank Matranga, was commissioned to create four murals portraying scenes from San Diego's history to be installed over the entry doors of a new Sears building on East Valley Parkway in the mid-1970s. When the building, which had also been occupied by the Fedco membership store from 1986 to 1989, was demolished in the early 1990s, the murals were saved. One, depicting a scene from the 1846 Battle of San Pasqual, can be seen today on the front of the Children's Discovery Museum at 320 North Broadway while another can be found on a median wall along South Date Street.

Queen Califia's Magical Circle is the only American sculpture garden and the last major international project created by French artist Niki de Saint Phalle, one of the most significant female and feminist artists of the twentieth century. Inspired by California's mythic, historic and cultural roots, the garden is located at Kit Carson Park. In the photograph, taken at her home where the maquette was displayed, stands Niki de Saint Phalle with her arm raised and to her immediate right, Mayor Lori Holt Pfeiler. *Don E. Anderson photograph.*

Since the Public Art Program began in 1988, more than 22 public art projects have been initiated by the City of Escondido and private developers. The Public Art Program has received a number of local and national awards for its projects.

This bronze fountain at the right, designed by James Hubble in 1989, is a memorial to Joyce and Irvin Malcolm, prominent supporters of the arts and the preservation of Escondido. It can be found at Trinity Episcopal Church, 9th Avenue and Chestnut Street.

In 2000, Wick Alexander created *Pillars of the Community* in multiple locations along South Escondido Boulevard. The entire Public Arts project included nine obelisks, three murals, and sundials and historic street names incised into the surface of the sidewalks. The obelisks, like the one at the left, start at the southeast corner of 6th Avenue and end at the southeast corner of 15th Avenue.

The mural at right with a self-guided walking tour of historic homes that had been located at the corner of Escondido Boulevard and 8th Avenue fell into disrepair and was removed in 2017.

Located in the Maple Street Plaza, between Grand Avenue and West Valley Parkway, artist Paul Hobson created a fountain and curved seat wall to celebrate the importance of Escondido Creek. The risers in the water feature were inspired by historic agricultural flood irrigation. *Brad Ansley photograph.*

Military Tribute, created by Gale Pruitt in 2007, is one of several veterans memorials in Grape Day Park. Bronze statues depict a female fighter pilot representing Women Air Force Service Pilots of World War II; a tall male soldier symbolizing those currently in combat; and a youthful ROTC student representing the future. The statues are flanked by the Walls of Courage, inscribed with names of local veterans.

Community was created by Jeff Lindeneau in 1990 as one of the early public art pieces.. Two cast bronze triangles featuring silhouettes of human figures stand atop two copper clad and granite slabs, facing each other, connoting a passage way.

Also created as a Public Art project, the *2011 New Leaf* by artist Dan Dykes is located on South Centre City Parkway near Felicita Avenue. According to the artist, the green patina represents Escondido's agricultural past, the stainless steel represents modern manufacturing, and the stainless-steel mesh at the top symbolizes the history of Escondido, coming together to form a new leaf.

Performing Arts

The annual Felicita Pageant featured 200 local thespians and was held from 1927-1932 in the Quiet Hills area near Felicita Park in south Escondido. The play was written by Benjamin Sherman, a local optometrist, and based on Elizabeth Judson Robert's book, *Indian Stories of the Southwest*. The pageant attracted hundreds of guests every year to sit under a canopy of oak trees while viewing the play. This photograph was taken during the 1930 production.

In 1923, *The Tom Thumb Wedding* was performed by a group of children at the Kinema Theater on Grand Avenue. In 1935, the children of the Methodist Church performed in a similar production, taking the roles normally played by adults.

This photograph was taken on April 14, 1916 and shows the cast of the Escondido High School production of Gilbert and Sullivan's, *H.M.S. Pinafore*. The operetta took place at the school in the Robert's Auditorium and the special scenery was produced by the Art Department. Although the operetta story-line centers around the British Navy, it's interesting to note that American flags were used in the production.

The first Patio Playhouse opened with its first play in 1971 in this remodeled machine shop on Hale Avenue. The founders sought to provide a creative outlet for talent, young and old, and to bring live theater to the community. The founders were Curtis Babcock; Dale Baldridge, and Greg and Don Krueger. Today, it is the oldest continuously-operating community theater in San Diego County.

Georgia Copeland, a former MGM starlet who danced in numerous musical movies, opened her dance studio in Escondido in 1953, making it the oldest dance studio still operating in North San Diego County today. Georgia personally produced more than 40 professional dancers in the course of her teaching career. When Georgia died in 1998, Sue Gibson assumed the operation of the studio. The snapshot shows Georgia on the left and Sue Gibson on the right. *Photograph courtesy of Georgia's Dance Studio*

This aerial photograph shows the California Center for the Arts under construction in April 1992, located just west of Grape Day Park, along Escondido Boulevard. Escondido voters approved spending $73 million to build the Center that would bring music, dance, theater, education and the visual arts together on one dynamic campus as part of an overall redevelopment project.

The completed Center for the Arts, Escondido, is shown in this September 1994 photograph.

The Kinema Theatre opened at the 200 block of east Grand Avenue in December 1920 and is featured in this photograph from 1929. The Kinema hosted Escondido's first motion pictures with sound and was the place of many community gatherings. In 1931 it became known as the Pala Theater.

The Ritz Theater, near the southeast corner of Grand Avenue and Juniper Street opened during the Grape Day Festival in 1937. In 1950, a fire damaged much of the interior and this photograph from 1952 shows the wood barricades in the doorways prior to its re-opening in 1953. The theater managed to stay open for a time, then closing and re-opening multiple times under a succession of owners until it closed for the final time in 2003. The Grand Market, in the companion building next door on the corner with similar art deco features, was the first grocery store in the city to have wheeled shopping carts. In 2015, it would become an Arthur Murray Dance Studio.

On June 19, 1950, a 2,080-pound replica of the Liberty Bell visited Escondido. The bell was one of 52 replicas donated to the U.S. Treasury by America's copper industry. The visit was part of a state-wide tour being made in connection with "Independence Drive," a program to increase the sales of U.S. Saving Bonds. The photograph shows the procession in front of the Pala Theater, which was located near the corner of Grand Avenue and Kalmia Street. Shortly after this photograph was taken, the theatre was converted into an eight-lane bowling alley, Pala Bowl.

The Escondido Drive-In opened on July 6, 1950, at 755 West Mission Avenue and the price of admission for that night's feature, *The Boy from Indiana*, was 50 cents. California political hopeful and future President, Richard Nixon, made a campaign stop at the drive-in that same year, and in 1962, a local pastor began holding Sunday worship services in the lot. The drive-in could accommodate about 320 cars and films such as 1959's *Ben Hur* sold out several times each night. The owner, Dan Johnston, moved the drive-in to West Mission Avenue in 1967 to accommodate the thriving business. This drive-in closed September 8, 1985.

In 2000 and 2001, Escondido's last two movie theaters closed, forcing residents to drive to theaters in San Marcos or Oceanside to see new movies on the "big screen." The community was pleased to have a local theater again, when a new 16-screen multiplex with stadium seating, shown in the 2018 photo, opened on January 30, 2004, at the site of the old Montgomery Ward store on the corner of Valley Parkway and Escondido Boulevard.

Literature

Harold Bell Wright was a best-selling American writer of fiction, essays, and nonfiction. Although mostly forgotten or ignored after the middle of the twentieth century, he is said to have been the first American writer to sell a million copies of a novel and the first to make $1 million from writing fiction. From 1935 until his death in 1944, Wright lived on his "Quiet Hills" farm in south Escondido. Two of his most popular novels are: *Shepard of the Hills* and *The Winning of Barbara Worth*.

Frances Beven Ryan taught home economics in Escondido schools for thirty years and then wrote several books about Escondido history, based on stories told to her by her relatives, who were among Escondido's founders and first settlers; *Early Days in Escondido* (1970), *Yesterdays in Escondido* (1973), and *Escondido As It Was* (1980). She also wrote a weekly history column for the *Times-Advocate*. The Escondido Library Pioneer Room was established as a bequest by Ryan in 1992. In the photograph from 1971, she is seen handing one of her books to then Mayor Allen Skuba while William Fark sits to the right and her husband, Lewis, stands by her side at the dedication of the recently relocated original library.

Another Escondido native, William Maurice Culp, whose uncle was the town marshal for a time, wrote several childrens books, including *Tumba of Torrey Pines* in 1931, *Jeremiah* in 1932, as well as *And a Duck Waddles Too* in 1939.

Museums

The San Diego Children's Discovery Museum provides hands-on educational exhibits and programs focusing on science, art, and world cultures for children. In 1999, it was founded by local resident Katie Ragazzi as a traveling education program in science and art. The following year, it incorporated as the Escondido Children's Museum. In 2001, the doors to the first museum facility opened in a small storefront on Grand Avenue. Three years later, it moved to a larger venue on the campus of the California Center for the Arts Escondido. With the opening of its third and current location on North Broadway, the Escondido Children's Museum changed its name to San Diego Children's Discovery Museum.

Keith Roynon began collecting his first fossils as a young child and, in 2000, began inviting school children to his home where his large collection was displayed. After a complaint was filed in March 2015, the City notified Roynon that the residence could no longer open its doors for the thousands of students who came every year. Community volunteers quickly intervened, finding and renovating acceptable quarters in a storefront on Grand Avenue to house Roynon's entire collection of more than 4,000 artifacts. The Roynon Museum of Paleontology was voted "Best Museum in the San Diego area" for 2016, according to the San Diego A-List website but would close in 2019 due to operational challenges.

Chapter 5
Government Sites and Services

Escondido was incorporated in 1888 as a result of a 64-19 vote by city residents, who also elected the first members of the Board of Trustees. The Board met monthly, upstairs at 110 West Grand. In 1930, the Board of Trustees became the City Council and the chairman became the mayor. In 1955, an ordinance was adopted, setting up the current Council-Manager form of government.

A Public Library was Escondido's first city service. In the early 1900s, the city also began paving roads. The Parks and Recreation Dept. was formed in 1956, later to become part of the Community Services Department. Escondido has always offered a wide variety of outdoor recreational opportunities, including camping, fishing, picnicking, hiking, and boating. Currently, the City maintains Dixon Lake, Lake Wohlford, Daley Ranch, and nine urban parks.

The scope of city services has steadily increased over the years, particularly as the city limits extended outward and the population grew. Eleven different departments, in addition to the City Manager's, City Attorney's, City Treasurer's, and City Clerk's offices, now provide residents with a wide range of services.

Escondido has experienced very few major crimes that have attracted national attention. Sadly, a post office shooting in 1989 became the second postal shooting in the country, followed by others in different cities that led to the term "going postal." Also receiving national attention was the murder in 1998 of Stephanie Crowe, who was stabbed multiple times in her bedroom. Another tragic murder

In celebration of the City's Centennial, a time capsule was buried under the center of the dome of the new City Hall and covered by a bronze marker. City employees Jerry Chappel (left) and Dave Cramer (right), are shown installing the time capsule in this 1988 photograph.

occurred in 2009, when Amber DuBois was abducted on her way to school. Her murder, and Chelsea King's of Rancho Bernardo, by the same man, led to the passing of Chelsea's Law, which, among other provisions, increased penalties, parole provisions, and oversight for violent sexual predators who attack children.

Fires have taken lives as well as damagied and destroyed property throughout Escondido's history. Thankfully, however; the number of fires has steadily decreased, thanks to stricter fire codes, including mandated fire sprinklers in new construction, as well as more advanced firefighting equipment and strategies. The Fire Department also began offering medical aid and transport in 1977 with those calls now making up 80 percent of fire department calls while fire-related calls constitute only 1.7 percent of their nearly 16,000 annual calls.

Buildings

By 1890, the first dedicated City Hall was located on Grand Avenue and a small building to the rear served as the City jail. Note the sunrise decoration above the windows and doors; similar detail adorns the front of the current City Hall.

A City Hall built of adobe block and made possible by the Works Progress Administration (WPA), was finished in 1938, in time to celebrate the city's fiftieth anniversary. It housed city offices, including the Police Department, and the Fire Station, which was added onto the north side a year later. The building was located on what is now the front lawn of the vacated Palomar Hospital, downtown, where Valley Parkway and Grand split.

In 1988, a new 108,000-square-foot City Hall was built at the corner of Valley Parkway and Broadway. The design was chosen by a public process, and a nation-wide competition was held. The 108 entries were reviewed by 1500 citizens and, using their comments, a jury chose the design submitted by Pacific Associates Planners and Architects, a San Diego firm. The building won several prestigious awards, including the Urban Land Institute Award for Excellence in 1989. This photograph shows the building's dedication ceremony with Mayor Doris Thurston at the podium.

Escondido's first Public Library was built in 1894 and the City assumed responsibility for its operation in 1898. The first librarian was Mina Ward and she was initially responsible for more than 300 books, all donated by the community. The building was moved to Grape Day Park in 1971 and now houses the Escondido History Center offices and research center.

On March 25, 1910, the cornerstone was laid for the Carnegie Library, which opened in October of that year. Books could be checked out every day except Sunday, when the library was open for quiet reading only, to honor the Sabbath. Businessman and philanthropist, Andrew Carnegie, donated money for building libraries around the world; 2,509 libraries were built between 1883 and 1929. This photograph is from a 1938 time capsule located at the adobe city hall and opened in 1988.

Also outgrown, the Carnegie Library was replaced in 1956 by this building on the left, designed by popular architect George Lykos. The strong example of Mid-century Style, named for art and culture advocates, Bob and Ruth Mathes, still stands at the northwest corner of Kalmia Street and 3rd Avenue.

Its distinctive light-controlling louvers recently removed, the Mathes Center continues to house meeting rooms and the Pioneer Room, which was established in 1992 with local historian Frances Beven Ryan's collection and other historical and genealogical research material.

In 1981, the 40,000-square-foot library was built next door and is still in use with more than 1,000 visitors daily. A major renovation was performed in 2009 to better accommodate today's technological needs and make it more attractive to visitors. In a controversial move, the City Council voted 4-1 to privatize the library services in 2017.

Chapter 5 ✦ 103

Parks

Grape Day Park was the city's first park, donated to the city to celebrate Grape Day, beginning in 1908. This photograph from 1976 shows the welcome sign and fountain, which still stand today. At one time, the park featured a bandshell and baseball fields as well as "the plunge," the first community pool.

The second oldest and largest in the county, this grand, multi-trunked eucalyptus tree sheltered Grape Day Park visitors for decades. Out of safety concerns, it was cut back significantly in 2013 with the tall stump remaining as a reminder of its earlier glory, while a design for its future use is being considered.

Nearby, when a restroom was needed for the Heritage Walk location, the last bid opened offered to do the job for only $1. Immediately accepted, the gazebo-shaped facility was completed by the community minded K. L. Wessel Construction Company.

"The Plunge" swimming pool in Grape Day Park was a popular place to cool off in the 1950s. A replacement municipal pool, built closer to Woodward Avenue, was named after Jim Stone, an Escondido High School teacher who worked as aquatics manager for the city during the summer. Stone was in charge of pool programs for more than twenty years.

James B. Dixon, superintendent of the Mutual Water Company, urged the City to build a dam, northeast of the city at this location, and the Dixon Lake Recreation Area was dedicated on May 12, 1977. The lake area continues to provide opportunities for fishing, camping, and picnicking. *Eric Johnson photograph.*

Robert Daley built a small cabin and settled in the valley around 1869. In 1925, he built a ranch house of single board, heart redwood that still stands today. In 1996, developer plans for the land surrounding it were halted when the Escondido City Council voted to purchase and forever protect the 3,058-acre ranch as a habitat preserve. Today, Daley Ranch offers more than 20 miles of trails for hiking, mountain bikes, and equestrian use and the ranch house is available for public use.

Named after the famous scout who also fought in the Battle of San Pasqual, the 285 acres where Kit Carson Park sits was purchased from the City of San Diego in 1967. One hundred acres have been developed into ball fields, tennis courts, and the Sports Center Complex. It's also the home of an amphitheater, Queen Califia's Magical Circle and the Iris Sanke Arboretum. The popular Escondido Rotary Club Disc Golf Course, depicted in this 2013 photograph, was established in 2010. The course meanders through a creek, oaks, alders, and manicured grass. 185 acres of Kit Carson Park have been preserved as natural habitat.

The photograph on the left, from January, 1952, shows Escondido Creek at a higher than average level, flowing through Grape Day Park. The City "Plunge" swimming pool can be seen toward the center back of the photograph. Flooding along Escondido Creek could be even more problematic.

In the 1960s, a flood control channel, shown in an early photograph on the right, was constructed to prevent flooding that occurred all too often throughout the community. The channel has been effective but not attractive, especially as it has collected trash, and the original wildlife habitat was greatly compromised.

In 2010, Landscape Architecture students at California State Polytechnic University, Pomona developed the "Revealing Escondido Creek Vision Plan." In it, all portions of the concrete drainage canal running through Escondido would be redesigned to return Escondido Creek to its more natural state while still retaining the ability to control flood waters as needed. As a result of that study, the City of Escondido began implementing the 100-acre linear park in phases.

In 2011, a portion of the Creek Trail was staged in conjunction with the grand opening of the adjacent Juniper Senior Village as shown in this photograph.

Deemed successful, the improvements were made permanent.

Law Enforcement

When Escondido was first incorporated, the town's law enforcement consisted of one man, who held the title of city marshal. In the photo, Marshal Luther Culp, who served from 1910 to 1916, is directing traffic on Grand Avenue. By 1956, the number of all law enforcement personnel stood at 15 but by 1986, the number had climbed to 125. Today there are 170 sworn police personnel, 93 non-sworn support personnel, and 73 volunteers.

After the new adobe City Hall at 100 Valley Boulevard was built in 1938, a small police headquarters and jail were constructed, also of adobe, north of and immediately adjacent to the City Hall. In this photograph from 1955, motorcycle officers are seen lined up for inspection by the police chief and the mayor behind City Hall.

In 1976, a new one-story Police Department headquarters, was built at 700 West Grand Avenue, while Lester R. Lund was Chief of Police. Plans had included a second floor but it was eliminated when city officials realized it would be too expensive, leaving two odd vertical features rising from the roof. When Lund became chief in 1956, the total department personnel numbered 15 in all ranks, but the population skyrocketed from 6,544 in 1950 to 64,355 in 1980 and the need for more police officers to provide service became obvious. By the time Lund retired in 1986, there were 125 employees. *Escondido Police Department Photograph.*

In 1982, to accommodate increasing staff numbers, a second floor was finally added to Police Headquarters at 700 West Grand Avenue and the look of the building was drastically different. It served for another 27 years until it was replaced in 2009 by a new facility shared with the Fire Department Administration on Centre City Parkway. *Escondido Police Department Photograph.*

Chapter 5 ♦ 109

In 2004, Proposition P was passed by the voters, providing $84.3 million to fund the construction of several fire stations and the construction of a $61 million combined state-of-the-art Police and Fire Headquarters building on Centre City Parkway. Shown in this photograph, groundbreaking for the 115,000-square-foot, three-story headquarters on Centre City Parkway at Decatur Way took place in September, 2006. The building was fully operational by May 2010.

Escondido is the only city in the county that has its own dispatch center for handling both police and fire emergency calls. This photograph, probably taken in the 1980s, shows Zelda White and Deanna Concannon at the far side of the room, handling emergency calls when it was located at the 700 West Grand Police Headquarters. *Escondido Police Department Photograph.*

Today's communications center, located in the more spacious Police and Fire Headquarters building, is staffed by 25 employees, working shifts to ensure that phones are answered 24/7 and 365 days per year. In the photo, Dispatcher Kim Rodriguez is viewing one of the five computer monitors at her station, typical for each of the dispatch stations in the center. In 2017, Dispatch answered more than 200,000 calls for service. *Escondido Police Department Photograph.*

A mounted police posse was formed by Police Chief Lloyd "Lefty" Mitchell in 1948, the first chartered mounted posse in the State of California. The Posse continues a fine tradition today, a popular riding group in local parades, including the Pasadena Rose Parade in 2012.

At one time, Escondido's small police force was bolstered by county deputy sheriffs stationed here, primarily to serve at the County Courthouse, located on East Valley Parkway. In October, 1958, Sheriff Deputy Neil Poole, who is pictured here, was involved in locating two bodies left by Harvey Glatman, the notorious "Glamour Girl Slayer," in the desert east of Escondido.

Fire Protection

In Escondido's earliest days, the town marshal would ring a hand bell along Grand Avenue when smoke was detected, replaced by a large bell at City Hall in 1892. Firefighting equipment consisted of a two-wheeled cart with a garden hose wrapped around a central cylinder, pulled by anyone who could respond; the original cart is shown in this photograph.

This 1914 Federal fire truck, with a maximum speed of twenty miles per hour, was the volunteer fire department's first motorized piece of equipment. When it was overwhelmed during a major fire that destroyed the Escondido Vineyard and Winery Company on the west side of town in 1926, funds were allocated for a 1926 La France fire truck with a 500-gallon water tank. Leather helmets and canvas turnout coats were purchased at the same time. In 1922, a 20-man volunteer fire department was established.

In 1939, the first fire station was constructed on the north side of the year-old city hall. The two-story structure included a brass pole to speed the firefighters' descent to the first floor. By 1953, the former all-volunteer Fire Department had two paid firefighters who alternated 24-hour shifts.

The position of fire chief wasn't full time until 1958 when 18 full-time firefighters were hired and a Fire Prevention Bureau was established. This photograph was taken in 1987, the year before the fire station was demolished along with the old City Hall.

In 1961, a new main fire station with administrative offices was built on Quince north of Valley Parkway. It was heavily remodeled twice in its lifetime and demolished and replaced in 2008. By 1984, there were five fire stations in Escondido and two more by 2009.

In addition to the new Police/Fire Headquarters, Proposition P funding also provided for the construction of three fire stations and for the rebuilding of Fire Station 1 on Quince Avenue, which opened in September 2009. The 28,340-square-foot facility includes a state-of-the-art six-story training ground with tower.

The city's first major fire occurred in 1929 when the first high school, then located at 3rd Avenue and Hickory Street, burned to the ground. Flames could be seen from at least as far as Poway. Unfortunately, the new 1926 La France fire engine, now on display at Fire Station 1, broke down and was unable to be used to fight the fire.

Working in an area completely surrounded by wildland areas, Escondido fire crews have fought numerous fires in rough terrain and with development pushing outward from the city, wildland/urban interface fires have meant defending increasing numbers of homes located there. The fire in this photograph, looking west, shows a brush fire near Lake Hodges Dam in November 1944.

Flame (below) was a tiny puppy who became the last animal to be rescued from the tragic Humane Society fire (right) in January 2001. Approximately 85 animals were rescued overnight, but Flame had been overlooked in the darkness and wasn't brought out from the rubble until the following morning, 11 hours after the fire had started. The tragic fire, which killed at least 100 animals, garnered international attention and Flame was featured in an interview on the *Today Show*.

Adopted by the department's Public Education Specialist, Flame made several public appearances to teach fire safety behaviors before taking an early retirement.

The two-alarm fire was determined to have been the result of arson, although an intensive investigation never uncovered the identity of the perpetrator. *Flame's photo by Julia Escamilla.*

Chapter 5 ♦ 115

The events of 9/11 deeply affected our nation, and Escondido mourned the loss of our own Juan Pablo Cisneros, a beloved 24-year-old graduate of Orange Glen High School, who perished in the North Tower of the World Trade Center as a result of the terrorist attack. In response to the unprecedented loss of emergency responders, a small group of Escondido firefighters climbed into a borrowed motorhome with a supply of custom-printed T-shirts to sell and drove across country, collecting more than $250,000 from communities along the way. When they reached New York City, the firefighters presented a check and connected personally with families and friends of the firefighters who had perished. Shown in this photograph of the firefighters being blessed by the Police Department Chaplain are, (from left to right) Chris Sovay, Chaplain Pat Kenney, Mike O'Connor, Eric Souza, Mike Bertrand, and Mike Diaz.

Escondido firefighter Pete Ordille, standing upright in the center of the photograph, was part of the Federal Emergency Management Agency Urban Search and Rescue team from San Diego, sent to New York City to work in the aftermath of 9/11. Deployed from September 17 until October 8, they worked "the pile" in 12-hour shifts. *Pete Ordille photograph*

The Witch Creek Fire of 2007 started east of Julian and combined with the Guejito Fire in the San Pasqual Valley, spreading nearly to the coast, and burning more than 197,990 acres and killing 2 people. The fires triggered the largest evacuation in county history with more than 500,000 people evacuated and a final total cost of $1.339 billion. The Witch Creek and Guejito Fires were among twenty-one wildfires burning in Southern California at the time. *Escondido Fire Department photograph.*

The largest structure fire in the city's history destroyed four four-story condominium buildings under construction in downtown Escondido in 2007. The dry wood framing, much of it still surrounded by scaffolding, burned explosively with 300-foot flames and a 1,000-foot tall column of smoke visible from as far as the coast. The active fire continued from early afternoon until well into the night. A total of 100 firefighters responded along with 25 engines, including all five of Escondido's and 20 others from across North San Diego County. Damage was estimated at $6 million. *Troy Burlington photograph.*

The city's second four-alarm fire occurred in 2017 when the abandoned historic Talone's meat market and slaughter house on Hale Avenue, next to the I-15 Freeway, burned to the ground and presented a risk to the Sprinter light rail line. *Escondido Fire Department photograph*

Chapter 5 ✦ 117

Escondido Timeline

1000 BC-1700 AD
First people in area were the Kumeyaay Indians

1843 Governor Micheltorena granted Escondido Valley to Juan Bautista Alvarado, who named the 12,653 acres "El Rincon del Diablo."

1846 Battle with Mexico fought at San Pasqual, December 6, 1846

1847 Treaty of Guadalupe Hidalgo

1850 California became a state

1855 After Alvarado died, his descendants started selling off his land and Judge Oliver Witherby of San Diego began buying portions of El Rincon del Diablo. It took him 10 years to purchase the entire ranch.

1868 Nathaniel Harrison, a freed slave, homesteaded on the side of Palomar Mountain. Witherby sold Rancho del Diablo to John, Josiah, and Matthew Wolfskill and Ed McGeary for $8,000.

1870 Zena Sikes built his adobe home (across Bear Valley Parkway from today's Westfield Shoppingtown, North County)

1883 Valley purchased by the Stockton Company, a group formed by fifteen men from Central California. They planted grapes next to the Escondido Creek. It rained fifty inches which was too much for the grapes.

1884 Post office name changed from Apex to Escondido.

1885 The Thomas brothers came to California. Five of the brothers, Jacob Gruendike, and seven others formed the Escondido Land and Town Co. and purchased the 12,814-acre valley for $102,042.

1886 Construction began on the Escondido Hotel on the east end of Grand Avenue. The University of Southern California, with Methodist backing, was given land to build a church on Grand Avenue and a seminary at 3rd and Hickory. Graham & Steiner opened the first store in town. The *Escondido Times*, a local newspaper, began weekly publication. The Board of Trade was founded, renamed the Chamber of Commerce in 1895.

1887 Construction of the Oceanside-to-Escondido railroad line began in March 1887 and was completed in January 1888. The Lime Street School, in what would later become Grape Day Park, opened. The first stagecoach travelled between San Diego and Escondido.

1888 The City of Escondido was incorporated on October 8. It consisted of 1854 acres.

1890 Population: 541. Escondido Irrigation District proposed a $450,000 bond issue to build a reservoir.

1891 Grand Avenue, downtown, had at least 12 oil lights. *The Advocate*, the second newspaper in town, began publication.

1893 50,000 fruit trees were planted.

1894 Construction of Bear Valley Dam began. USC's seminary became Escondido High School.

1895 Bear Valley Dam completed. Water became available. City's first library built.

1900 Population: 755. Grove owners formed the Citrus Union within the decade.

1901 Street lights were changed from oil to gas.

1905 The water bonds were paid off on October 31. Grand Avenue received sidewalks.

1907 Two inches of snow fell in February and again in April. A movie theater opened. Escondido High School students dug a pool by hand, next to the school.

1908 The first official "Grape Day" was held on California Admission Day, September 9.

1909 Giant eucalyptus tree was planted in what will become Grape Day Park. Local newspapers, the *Escondido Times* and *The Advocate*, merged into *The Times-Advocate*.

1910 Population 1,334. The first electric service in town was available on March 5 from sundown until 10:00 p.m. The Lime Street School, the city's first, was torn down. Escondido Women's Club was organized. Carnegie Library replaced city's first library.

1911 Natural gas became available. In December, William Alexander bought the Escondido Land and Town Company.

1912 Grand Avenue was fully paved.

1914 Palm trees were planted on Grand Avenue from the train depot to Maple Avenue.

1915 Hotel Charlotta opened. Escondido Humane Society was organized.

1916 "Hatfield's Flood," 24.1 inches, ruins railroad tracks. No trains in or out of Escondido for a month.

1917 San Diego Gas & Electric purchased the Escondido Utilities Company and provided 24-hour service.

1918 Lake Hodges Dam was completed.

1920 Population: 1,789. Prohibition began, banning manufacture, sale, and transportation of alcohol while thousands of acres of grapes are being grown in Escondido.

1921 First service station started in town.

1922 A 20-man volunteer fire department was established.

1923 Escondido Hotel, built in 1886, is torn down. Escondido Hospital, the first in town, was opened on Grand Avenue by six doctors.

Escondido Timeline ✦ 119

1924 Escondido Dam and Lake becomes Lake Wohlford. Kiwanis and Rotary clubs form.

1927 Escondido High School moved into new building at the corner of Hickory Street and 4th Avenue. The Masons erected a flag pole in the middle of the street on Grand at Broadway. The Felicita Pageant debuted.

1928 Escondido Fruit Growers divided into Escondido Lemon Association and Escondido Orange Association. First commercial avocados planted.

1929 A. L. Houghtelin constructed a 50-foot-diameter wooden tepee, which became a local landmark for nearly 50 years. First Escondido High School burned down. Lemon packing house opened.

1930 Population: 3,421. Post office began home delivery of the mail. Many street names changed. The city's Board of Trustees changed their name to the City Council.

1931 Lake Hodges overflowed the first time.

1933 Charlotte Baker and Elizabeth Martin started the city's second hospital in a former egg and poultry business on the west side of Lime Street, now Broadway, just north of 2nd Avenue.

1936 WPA built an adobe band stand in Grape Day Park.

1938 Escondido celebrated its fifty-year anniversary. The second City Hall, built of adobe, opened at Grand and Valley.

1940 Population: 4,560.

1941 World War II troops camped in Grape Day Park.

1944 Flagpole on Grand Avenue at Broadway was removed.

1945   Local lemon production reached a peak, with 1,159,039 field boxes. Railroad passenger service between Escondido and Oceanside was discontinued.

1947   Escondido High School had its first night football game.

1948   Palomar Observatory was completed. Palomar Hospital District was formed.

1949   Highway 395 opened through town.

1950   Population: 6,544. Highway 395 to San Diego was opened. Palomar Hospital opened with 10 patients. Cora Swingle was the first woman elected to serve on City Council. The Ritz Theater was gutted by fire.

1951   The city's first annexation added 8.7 acres to the city.

1952   Ups N Downs Roller Rink opened. Kay Owens started Escondido's only radio station, KOWN.

1955   After a construction flaw in Escondido High School was discovered, the student body was divided, with some attending a new campus on North Broadway. The rest were taught in temporary classrooms on the original campus.

1956   New library at 3rd Avenue and Kalmia Street replaced the Carnegie Library. The Escondido Historical Society was established.

1959   Entire student body attended Escondido High School together again at North Broadway site.

1960   Population: 16,377. Lemon packing house closed.

1962   Orange Glen High School opened.

1964   Escondido Village Mall was built on East Valley Parkway.

1966   Medians were added to Grand Avenue. The first Escondido Drive-In opened.

1967   Four inches of snow fell in December. Patio Playhouse opened.

1969   Kit Carson Park was dedicated.

1970   Population: 36,792.

1971   Dixon Dam and Lake were dedicated. City's first library building was moved from Grand Avenue to Grape Day Park.

1972   San Pasqual High School opened. San Diego Zoo's Wild Animal Park opened.

1974   Lorraine Boyce was the first woman to be elected mayor.

1976   New Police Headquarters was built at 700 West Grand. Heritage Walk was established in Grape Day Park.

1977   Dixon Lake Recreation Area was dedicated. Escondido Auto Park was built. The Tepee, a large wooden structure and local landmark for nearly fifty years was blown down by the wind.

1980   Population: 64,355.

1981 Current library at Broadway and 2nd Avenue was built. Escondido Auto Park opened. Escondido National Little League All-Star team played in the Little League World Series in Pennsylvania.

1982 Rube Nelson's Country Corner grocery store closed.

1984 Santa Fe Depot was purchased from the Santa Fe Railroad Company and moved to Grape Day Park.

1986 North County Fair Shopping Center (currently Westfield North County), a regional shopping center, opened.

1988 Escondido celebrated its centennial. City personnel moved into a new City Hall at the corner of Broadway and Valley Parkway. Biannual Street Faire began.

1989 Downtown Farmers Market began in October

1990 Population: 108,635

1994 California Center for the Arts opened.

1995 East Valley Community Center opened. First Night began December 31, 1995. Escondido Arts Partnership was established.

1996 Grape Day Festival and Parade were revived. City purchased Daley Ranch.

2000 Population 133,630. Steve Waldron started the Cruisin' Grand event.

2001 Escondido Humane Society in Kit Carson Park burned down. Escondido Children's Museum opened on Grand Avenue.

2003 Queen Califia's Magical Garden by Nikki de Saint Phalle opened in Kit Carson Park. In October, firestorms raged. Mingei International Museum satellite opened downtown. Escondido Humane Society opened new facility on East Valley Parkway.

2004 Escondido Children's Museum moved to Studio One at the California Center for the Arts. "Vinehenge," public art that doubled as a playground opened in Grape Day Park.

2006 Escondido Historical Society celebrated its fiftieth anniversary with a name change to Escondido History Center

2007 Witch Creek fire destroyed more than 200,000 acres and caused two deaths. President Bush landed at San Pasqual High School to tour the devastation. Paramount Condominiums, under construction on Escondido Boulevard, burned down.

2008 Sprinter light rail system began running between Escondido and Oceanside.

2009 Final stage of the Amgen Race of California brought thousands of bicycle enthusiasts downtown.

2010 Population: 144,464 California State Polytechnic University, Pomona developed plan for "Revealing Escondido Creek" to create a linear park to ultimately replace most of the flood control channel.

2012 The new 740,000-square-foot, 11-story Palomar Medical Center on the west side of Escondido was opened.

2013 The first leg of the Amgen Race of California started in Escondido.

2014 Maple Street Plaza, a pedestrian mall with public art pieces opens across from City Hall. For the first time, four of the five City Council Members were elected from individual districts with the mayor elected by all city voters.

2015 After more than 50 years, most departments in the Palomar Medical Center downtown campus closed. The Roynon Museum of Earth Science and Paleontology opened to the public on Grand Avenue.

2016 New agriculture-themed playground area opened at Grape Day Park. EcoVivarium, a "living museum," featuring reptiles, amphibians, and arthropods opened to the public.

2017 Talone's meat market and slaughterhouse, vacant for several years, burned down.

2018 Signage added to History Center's Heritage Walk Buildings.

About the Authors

Robin Fox has worked for the Escondido History Center since 1998 and was appointed executive director in 2018. She grew up in Escondido, attending San Pasqual High School before attending Brigham Young University, where she received a degree in education. Robin was also awarded a certificate in archival management from the Western Archives Institute. With a deep understanding and appreciation of Escondido's history, Robin has cared for and taught our history to thousands of residents and visitors, alike. Robin is wearing a charming dress with lace-edged collar in this 1961 photograph.

Carol Rea has been fascinated by historic homes for most of her life. She came to Escondido in 1991 to work for the Escondido Fire Department and moved into her first historic home, located in the Old Escondido Historic District, in 2000. Not long after, she was appointed to the Old Escondido Board of Directors and, in 2008, became the President, a position she held until 2018 when she began volunteering with the Escondido History Center and was appointed to the its Board of Directors. After Carol retired from the Fire Department in 2009, she was appointed to the City's Design Review Board as the expert in Historic Preservation and later to the Historic Preservation Commission, where she has served as Chairman for the last four years. Note the array of fine beauty products displayed behind Carol, who was styling in her favorite cowgirl look, in this drug store photograph, from 1957.

About the Cover

Artist Gloria Warren has always had a special fondness for painting historic California scenes and the challenges they present. Though raised in the cities of New York and Los Angeles, married life brought her to San Diego's back country and the many new and challenging painting opportunities nature provides.

www.ingramcontent.com/pod-product-compliance
Lightning Source LLC
Chambersburg PA
CBHW040800240426

43673CB00015B/405